STRICTLY STRESS

**Effective
Stress
Management**

GW00585822

A series of 12
sessions for
High School
Students

Tina Rae

Reprinted 2003, 2007

Paul Chapman Publishing
A SAGE Publications Company
1 Oliver's Yard
55 City Road
London EC1Y 1SP

SAGE Publications Inc.
2455 Teller Road
Thousand Oaks, California 91320
SAGE Publications India Pvt Ltd
B-42, Panchsheel Enclave
Post Box 4109
New Delhi 110 017

ISBN 978-1-873942-14-7

Printed on paper from sustainable resources
Printed in Great Britain by Cromwell Press Ltd

Contents

How to use the CD-ROM

The CD-ROM contains PDF files, labelled 'Worksheets.pdf' which contain worksheets for each lesson in this resource. You will need Acrobat Reader version 3 or higher to view and print these resources.

The documents are set up to print to A4 but you can enlarge them to A3 by increasing the output percentage at the point of printing using the page set-up settings for your printer.

Alternatively, you can photocopy the worksheets directly from this book.

Introduction & Background

This programme is designed to be used in the Secondary phase with both groups of students and whole classes and can be delivered by school based staff working independently or in conjunction with the SENCO or an Outside Agency. It is specifically aimed at students who appear to be experiencing unacceptable levels of stress in their lives and require support in order to understand, acknowledge and cope with specific stressors/sources of stress. Such students may exhibit low self-esteem and levels of confidence alongside difficulties in asserting themselves. These difficulties may be part of more general emotional and behavioural difficulties which will also impact negatively upon learning and social interactions. These students will clearly benefit from this course which aims to support them in developing the skills and strategies they will need in order to cope effectively in a range of situations. However, students who are experiencing particular life changes such as death, divorce, change of school etc. or who have specific difficulties in organising themselves and their workloads - especially during exam periods - will also benefit from this series of lessons. (Since High School students will have to cope with the stress of examinations it could be argued that they would all perhaps benefit from such a course at some point in their school careers).

Defining the word stress is very difficult as it is person specific and, like the words happiness, failure or success, it can and does mean different things to different people (Hans Selye, 1974)

The term 'stress' was initially used in the 17th century to describe distress, oppression and hardship. Today the term covers a wide range of things, most of which appear to be unpleasant to the individuals/groups concerned. There seems to be some agreement on general areas and the fact that stress is a process of mental, physical and emotional reactions which are caused by a significant increase in pressures without the necessary level of coping resources or strategies. Stress can consequently be defined as any strain, pressure or force which prevents individuals from functioning efficiently.

Experiencing tension or stress is, however, a normal part of daily life. It is when individuals experience too much of either that they become tired, ill, anxious, exhausted and ultimately burnt out. Not experiencing manageable levels of tension of stress is also unhealthy as this simply results in the creation of unchallenged and unstretched individuals who lose the capacity to grow and effect change. Each individual can be said to have an optimum stress level which allows them to function effectively and efficiently. What is most important is to recognise our own satisfactory stress levels and to develop the coping strategies to maintain a healthy balance of tension, growth, test and self-nurturing. Appleby's (1967) Stress Thresholds diagram illustrates this point, showing how a comfortable level of stress promotes efficiency. It also highlights how sustaining peak performance is extremely difficult and how, at this level, it is all to easy to tip over into overloading oneself. It would consequently appear that most individuals would be wisest to function at just below their peak performance level.

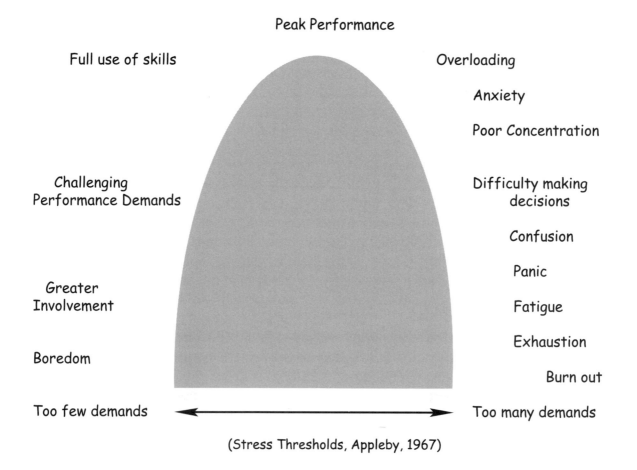

(Stress Thresholds, Appleby, 1967)

Perhaps most important in ensuring this balance is how the individual actually perceives the challenges that life brings. It is frequently our perceptions that can and do affect our health, self-esteem, morale and efficiency. Consequently, a central aim of this course is to ensure that students understand how seeing the positives can and does minimise stress. Such a philosophy is also supported by a focus on identifying reactions that both reduce and increase stress alongside an emphasis on understanding, acknowledging and coping effectively with the sources of our individual stressors. In developing such skills and knowledge students are also encouraged to feel that they themselves are in control of their own lives and that they can and should communicate their experiences, feelings and problems to others. It is through this process of communication that they will promote and increase both their own self-esteem and that of their friends/peers and family members.

Recognising the factors that cause stress and tension both generally and for the individual, is a prerequisite to change. However, it is important to highlight how certain sources of stress are harder to change than others. Some stressors may need to be managed or coped with whilst others may be impossible to change. It will not always be possible to remove a stressor entirely. The contents of the following stressor list perhaps reinforces this point.

- death of a parent or close relative
- break up of a relationship that the student is in
- peer pressure to take drugs / have sex
- divorce/the loss of a parent through divorce
- financial worries or problems

- death of a close friend
- rows between parents
- health issues such as surgery, pregnancy etc.
- marriage
- conflict
- unemployment
- sexual problems
- a lack of privacy
- deadlines
- a new job/school
- moving house
- insecurities regarding the future
- isolation from peer group
- exams or tests
- making decisions
- concerns about one's weight or appearance
- feelings of frustration.

Death of a parent or close relative is a stressor which the individual may well be able to cope with through time, but it cannot be removed - unlike tests or exams which are definitely over at a given point in time.

Stephen Murgatroyd (1982) and his colleagues suggest that there are 10 potential 'stressors' or 'crisis points' which are specific to adolescence. It is essential that these are acknowledged and understood by those seeking to support students at this point in their development. These stressors/crisis points are described as follows:

- a feeling that they are falling short of standards and expectations
- feelings of uncertainty and sometimes a fear of future choices
- feeling fragmented - not feeling that he/she is a 'whole' person and yet also not knowing how to achieve such a goal
- feeling too dependent upon others (particularly adults) and feeling unable to break free from such a dependence
- an unwillingness to set limits, even those that are known to be needed
- being unsure in the work situation or in the future in a job
- uncertainty regarding sexual roles/behaviour
- difficulties in making and sustaining significant relationships
- difficulties in coping with the range of emotions rising from our consciousness
- finding difficulty in accepting responsibility.

Clearly, this course has not been designed to specifically cover each of these crisis points in turn and cannot offer any conclusive solution to such a range of often existential issues. However, in line with John Colemen's (1990) suggestion that the majority of adolescents tend to focus on one 'stressor' at a time, this course does allow students to develop their own crisis management skills and aims to provide them with a range of strategies and approaches in order to cope with these stressors more effectively and also to become more reflective, realistic and considered in their responses to stress.

Objectives

The lessons in this programme have been designed to meet the following objectives:

- to increase self-esteem/self-concept
- to enable students to understand how positive thinking and a positive attitude towards change can minimise stress
- to understand the nature and causes of stress in both general and personal terms
- to understand how stress is person-specific
- to increase co-operation and empathy
- to enable students to recognise their own optimum stress levels which allow for efficient functioning
- to recognise reactions and behaviours which both reduce and increase stress
- to understand and recognise the consequences of a range of stress in both themselves and others
- to develop joint problem solving skills within a supportive framework
- to encourage an understanding of how others view us and how this can/may impact upon both our self-esteem and our ability to cope with stress and tension in everyday life
- to identify and develop a range of personal strategies to manage personal stressors
- to understand the importance of emotional support from significant others (friends/family etc.) in coping effectively with stress
- to understand how a healthy lifestyle can reduce stress / enable us to cope more effectively with a range of stressors
- to develop the ability to prioritise and organise both work and social agendas and to understand how this skill can reduce stress
- to understand the difference between aggression and assertion
- to develop and practice assertiveness skills, understanding how such skills can aid in the management of stress
- to understand how stress can adversely affect muscles and breathing and how making use of progressive relaxation can reduce such symptoms
- to increase student's level of confidence in social interactions and in their own ability to cope with a range of more stressful situations and conflicts
- to develop skills of reflection
- to enable students to set realistic and considered personal goals
- to improve student's ability to manage and cope effectively with stress and to consequently reduce current stress levels and anxieties.

The Structure of the Programme

The programme is structured as follows:

Introductory Session
One to one interviews with students who will be included in the programme. The interview adopts a Brief Therapy approach in order to identify individual needs and stressors and to develop appropriate targets via the formulation of an Anti-Stress plan.

Session 1
Group roles are set and agreed by all participants in this session. Students complete the Individual Stress Profile in order to identify current stressors and concerns. Key stressors are highlighted via the Stress Target sheet and student's personal targets are again reinforced. Students sign a Contract to Change which commits them to learning and adopting new coping strategies and skills introduced in the course.

Session 2
Identifying the nature and causes of stress via a Brainstorming Activity. Students rank a range of stressful situations and discuss the extent to which stress may be person specific. Students consider a range of case studies, identifying the character's main stressors and attempting to formulate useful and practical advice as to how these can be alleviated.

Session 3
Students co-operate in identifying the kinds of stress that young people may experience both in and out of the school context. Positive and negative reactions to these stressors are identified and acted out via the use of Role Play cards.

Session 4
The characteristics of a 'true friend' are identified and agreed. Students also identify their personal Circle of Friends and social support, highlighting how their friends can and do help them in stressful situations. The Stress Problem Page provides an opportunity to adopt the role of a 'true friend' in providing considered responses and advice to each request.

Session 5
Students clarify the nature of a healthy lifestyle and how this can be maintained. Completion of a 'How Healthy Are You Quiz' identifies personal health ratings and ways in which health can be improved and the direct link between a healthy lifestyle and the ability to cope effectively with stress.

Session 6
Distinguishing between aggressive, assertive and passive behaviours also allows students to identify behaviours that are likely to be the cause of the highest and lowest levels of stress. A self-evaluation exercise highlights the extent to which each individual adopts both assertive and aggressive responses to a range of situations and assess each other's performance by referring to the Assertive Behaviour Checklist.

Session 7

Students identify the need to be organised in order to alleviate stress and prevent situations becoming stressful. The opportunity to prioritise daily activities and create a daily plan of action reinforces the necessary skills. Developing a weekly timetable for a student also highlights the need to ensure a good balance between school, homework, leisure and rest.

Session 8

Brainstorming how and when students can relax and how these strategies may be person-specific begins this session. Students are encouraged to identify a personal haven and to make use of a relaxation script alongside drawing up a relaxation timetable for the week ahead.

Session 9

This session introduces 4 basic ways to handle stress: showing our feelings, self-nurturing, problem solving and being actively distracted. Students work with peers to problem solve personal stresses and a 4 step approach to solving problems is introduced and practised.

Session 10

Students devise their personal 'stress o' graph' on a daily basis in order to identify specific causes of stressful moments and to develop future coping strategies. A more in depth analysis of personal stressors is then encouraged and students work in small groups to formulate 'Stress Busters' for a range of problems.

Course Review

Students articulate knowledge and skills learnt from the course and evaluate their own progress to date, alongside also evaluating the resources provided in the course. All students are awarded the Certificate of Completion and are encouraged to share their successes in the group.

Success Criteria

It is hoped that the success of the Strictly Stress Course can be measured in the following areas:

- prompting school staff to reflect upon their practices and how these may impact upon student's behaviour, self-esteem and social and emotional development - particularly in terms of developing personal coping strategies and problem solving skills
- prompting a review of policies on self-esteem and emotional support for pupils in order to further develop more inclusive whole school approaches
- to identify any staff and pupil training needs in the areas of emotional awareness, mentoring, stress and anger management, assertiveness skills and basic counselling approaches
- enabling students to develop a more in depth awareness of and understanding of their own feelings, attitudes and behaviours
- encouraging students to reflect more specifically upon their own feelings and behaviours, being able to recognise and articulate both negative and positive patterns
- increasing students self-esteem/self-concept
- for students to understand and articulate the nature and causes of stress in

both personal and more general terms and to acknowledge the fact that stress is person-specific

- for students to understand how positive thinking can minimise stress and make appropriate use of this strategy
- increasing confidence, listening skills, assertive behaviours, co-operation and empathy
- to increase student's ability to recognise their own and others optimal stress levels and the reactions and behaviours which both increase and reduce stress
- for students to understand the importance of emotional support, a healthy lifestyle, the development of organisational skills and relaxation techniques and assertiveness skills in coping effectively with stress and to make use of this range of strategies in the process
- to enable students to develop skills of reflection and consequently to develop and set realistic personal goals and targets
- removing the risk of students suffering from extreme levels of stress and withdrawing from the school context
- for students to be able to develop the ability to transfer the skills and strategies taught into a range of social contexts.

Confidentiality – An important note

It is essential that students who participate in the Strictly Stress course feel safe, comfortable and secure in the knowledge that their contributions will be treated with respect and in confidence. When setting up the group and formulating and agreeing a set of group rules, all involved need to be made aware of the necessity to keep conversations private to the group. Divulging other's views / problems outside the group would simply be a total betrayal of trust and damage the self esteem and confidence of those involved. The course tutor will need to explicitly state that such behaviour will not be tolerated. Any students who chose to break this rule would, as a consequence, be required to give up their place on the course. Although this may appear somewhat harsh, it is essential to maintain such a position if all the students are to benefit from the group problem solving work and to develop the stress management skills that they need within a truly supportive framework.

Looking Ahead - Continuation of Support

Once students have completed the Strictly Stress Course it may be necessary to continue to monitor progress and to provide access to an appropriate support system. This may include ongoing Mentoring or involvement of Outside Agencies. Clearly, whatever decisions are made, the individual needs and requirements of the students will need to be carefully assessed at this point. Many of the students who will have been targeted via the course will have certainly appreciated the increase in their access to real 'Listening Time'. A Mentoring Scheme would at least continue to ensure weekly one-to-one sessions during which students could discuss specific stress related problems that they have encountered and will ensure that they have a confidential forum in which to problem solve and further develop their Stress Management Skills.

The Mentoring approach could, in turn, also form the basis of a whole school policy and approach to listening time which may well include the setting up of peer support groups i.e. self-help groups which focus on sharing and developing stress management skills. This would necessarily have resource and training implications i.e. training for staff and pupils in basic counselling skills, a review of the P.S.H.E Curriculum, setting up of Mentoring programmes and the creation of specific listening environments.

However school staff decide to support students in terms of developing social, emotional and academic skills (and specifically in developing stress management strategies), it will be necessary to ensure that the curriculum is both flexible and carefully designed to ensure the inclusion and emotional wellbeing of all students. It is hoped that this programme will reinforce the need for such an approach and perhaps also prompt staff to review and further develop their practices in terms of ensuring that all students develop all the skills that they need in order to cope effectively with their lives and the emotional, social and academic stresses and pressures that they may encounter.

STRICTLY STRESS

Introductory Session

- Initial one to one interviews with individual students
- Developing an Anti-Stress plan

Individual Session : 1 hour

The Interview

This initial session consists of a one to one interview between each participant and the course tutor. The interview should last approximately 1 hour. The main aim of the session is to begin to encourage the student to focus upon those things that work and to consequently feel able to set achievable targets in order to decrease levels of personal stress. Some clarification of the practical resources and strategies required by the students should also be possible at this stage.

The interview should take places in a quiet and comfortable room. The confidential nature of the interview should be made apparent at the onset i.e. the student's news, thoughts and feelings will not be fed back to staff or carers unless at the express wish of the individual student concerned. The obvious exception to this rule would be if students disclosed themselves to be at risk in any way and this should be clarified with students at the outset of this process.

The interview adopts a solution focused brief therapy approach. This focuses upon the visualisation of solutions as opposed to the exploration of problems. The session should also allow for the course tutor and each student to begin to develop a positive relationship within a comfortable and safe context. The tutor will make use of the Strictly Stress Initial one to one interview format in order to record student responses in note form. The interview is divided into 3 parts as follows:

Part 1
This part of the form focuses on the following questions:

- What is currently going well for you at school? Why?
- What is currently not going so well at school? Why?
- What is currently going well at home? Why?
- What is currently not going quite so well at home? Why?
- What do you think might help you at home/school?

The aim here is to identify positive and negative aspects of both contexts and to begin to articulate main areas of stress and any initial ideas as to what strategies, techniques or resources might begin to alleviate theses stressors.

Part 2
The student is then asked the Miracle Question and requested to imagine themselves in a situation in which all their problems, stressors and difficulties are 'solved'. The student is asked to describe a 'perfect day' in which everything goes well at home and at school. The question is framed as follows:
'Imagine that you go to bed tonight and a miracle happens - something or someone waves a magic wand over you and all your problems and difficulties are solved. You wake up to a perfect stress-free day - at home and at school. What is different? THINK - How does your day begin and then go on? Talk through 'what happens on this ideal/magic day.'

The Miracle Question is posed in order to enable the students to visualise 'Life without the problem' (de Shazer 1988, Furman and Ahola, 1992). In talking about 'life without the problem' students should begin to feel able to articulate ideas as to how they might begin to make specific changes. Realistic and achievable personal goals should then be formulated with greater ease and confidence. When posing the Miracle Question, it is important that the tutor emphasises the fact that this ideal day does not preclude the student from attending school. The aim here is to encourage students to describe school as they would really like it to be. This will enable them to reflect upon the differences between the ideal and the reality and to consequently articulate the changes that may need to be made alongside identifying the resources that they might need in order to effect these changes.

Part 3

The Scaling Activity next provides students with a visual image by which they can identify where they feel they 'are at' and how they may be able to move on from this particular point. These solution focused procedures which have been adopted in both the Scaling Activity and the initial parts of the individual interview are described by Rhodes and Ajmal in their book 'Solution Focused Thinking in Schools'. Adopting this approach is crucial and the reasons for doing so are made clear by the authors:

> 'In supporting students, teachers and parents in their wish to change what is happening, we have found no model.........more useful and flexible than solution focused thinking. It enables a different story to be told, one which emphasises the skills, strengths and resources of those involved.'
>
> Rhodes, J & Ajmal, Y. (1995) P.55.

The Scaling Activity asks the students to rate themselves on a scale of 0-10. 0 indicating that they feel extremely stressed and unable to currently cope effectively with life in general, 5 indicating that they feel reasonably happy but did not consistently make use of effective stress management strategies. A rating of 10 would imply that the student had no difficulties whatsoever i.e. life is perfect!

The rating/scaling system will clearly need to be explained in such terms to each student prior to starting the activity. Once they have identified this personal rating, it should be possible for students to identify the positive strategies, feelings and behaviours that they feel have allowed them to make this rating. Even if a student has rated themselves at 2-3 on the Scale, it should be possible to articulate those things that they are currently doing in order to cope - even to a limited extent. In visualising where they would like to be in the future i.e. life without the problem, the students should be able to identify what they will have to do in order to get to this point and articulate personal targets/goals.

An Example - Billy

Billy felt totally stressed by a range of situations both in and out of school. He felt as if everyone and everything in his life were having a negative impact on him and couldn't see a way out. His Mum and Dad had recently split up and his Mum had moved away to a town on the South Coast. It was at least 2 hours journey by car to get there. He had stayed with his Dad because he had just started Year 11 and he was due to sit his G.C.S.E. mocks at the end of the Autumn term. His parents both thought that was the most sensible thing to do. Unfortunately, he'd been really shocked when his parents told him about their split as they had been very careful not to show any negative behaviours towards each other when he was around. They wanted everything to be civilised. Billy wished that they had screamed and shouted - at least he would have had some warning. He felt angry at both of them and furious that his Mum had moved so far away as he could rarely get to see her. Also, he and his Dad had to share the cooking and the cleaning and he resented this as he invariably ended up doing more than his Dad. He was feeling tired a lot and couldn't focus in lessons. He also wasn't putting as much effort into his work and he was getting behind in course work - to the extent that his Maths and English teachers had threatened to phone home. He knew that his Mum and Dad wouldn't get back together even though he had visualised them in a state of wedded bliss in his Miracle/Perfect Day.

However, he was able to identify some of the things he could do in order to make some of the necessary changes:

- talk to his Mum and Dad about how he felt and tell them the truth about the schoolwork situation
- tell his Head of Year how he was feeling and ask for some extra time for his course work i.e. his Head of Year to negotiate on his behalf with the subject teachers
- agree a fairer routine with Dad regarding the household chores (and stick to it)
- ask his Mum if she could come up and stay with her Mum (his Nan!) every other weekend so they could spend some time together
- talk to his best friend a bit more instead of shutting him out and attempting to cope with these stresses on his own
- write out a Catch up plan/timetable for his homework and course work.

Billy rated himself at a 4 on the Scaling Activity but felt that he could achieve a rating of 7 or 8 if he could reach the above targets.

My Anti-Stress Plan

Once the student has completed the interview and Scaling Activity, this format can be used to reinforce specific targets/personal goals. There is also an opportunity to identify the skills needed and also to consider what might go wrong in this process. The latter is an important consideration. Pre-empting is clearly a useful strategy i.e. even if things don't go to plan there are others around who can help to get you back on track. Visualising success and the changes actually happening concludes the Anti-Stress Plan - How will you know if your plan is working? What will happen?

An Example - Billy's Anti-Stress Plan

Billy's plan included the following responses:

- I want to feel less stressed at home and school. I want to catch up with my work. I want to see my Mum more often.
- I need to get better organisational skills. I need to talk about how I feel to my Mum and Dad and not shut out my friends. I need to stick to my plan.
- I can be honest with myself and my Mum and Dad as this will help me reach these goals.

- Two things might go wrong - the teachers might not help me and I might not be able to catch up with all my work.
- I can ask my Dad to help me if things go wrong and Mr. Jordache (head of year) and Brian and Donna.
- I will know if my plan is working because I will feel less stressed and tired, my work will be better and I'll see my Mum.

Resources

The following resources will be needed for this session:

- a quiet (private) room
- 1 hour approximately per individual student interview
- a photocopy of the Interview format per student
- a photocopy of the Scaling Activity per student
- a photocopy of the Anti-Stress Plan per student.

STRICTLY STRESS

Initial Interview

- Name
- Date of Interview
- Recorded by

Introductory Session
Part 1

a) What is currently going well for you at school?

Why?

b) What is currently not going quite so well at school?

Why?

c) What is currently going well at home?

Why?

d) What is currently not going quite so well at home?

Why?

e) What do you think might help you:

at home?

at school?

The Miracle Question

Part 2

a) Imagine that you go to bed tonight and a miracle happens – someone or something waves a magic wand over you and all your problems and difficulties are solved. You wake up to a perfect stress-free day – at home and at school.
What is different? THINK – How does your day begin and then go on? Talk through what happens on this ideal/magic day.

b) What is different to a 'usual day'? Lets think back and list the differences.

＊

＊

＊

＊

＊

＊

The Scaling Activity

Name

Year Group

The Scale

Highlight/Tick where you are now

0 1 2 3 4 5 6 7 8 9 10

Stop and Think!: Answer the Questions!

What have you done to get to this point?

Where would you like to get to on the scale?

How can you do this?

What are your TARGETS?

Introductory Session

My Anti-Stress Plan

Name   Year Group

Re-State you TARGETS

What do you want to achieve?

What skills do you need to work on?

What else can you do to achieve your targets?

What might go wrong?

Who can support you if things go wrong?

How will you know if your plan is working? What will happen?

Go For It!

STRICTLY STRESS

Session 1

- ◆ Group Rules
- ◆ Individual Stress Profile
- ◆ Stress Target Sheet & Contract Change

Session 1

Group Session 45 minutes - 1 hour.

It will be necessary for the course tutor(s) to provide the students with an outline of the Strictly Stress Course as an introduction to the series of sessions. The main objectives need to be reinforced so that the students fully understand the purpose of this programme. These will be as follows:

- to provide students with a confidential and supportive framework in which they can begin to reflect upon their feelings, behaviours and stress levels
- to allow each student to understand the nature and causes of stress in both themselves and others and to distinguish between positive and negative responses to stress
- to encourage an understanding about how stress is person-specific and how they can learn to appreciate that people will need different levels of support at different times in their lives
- to enable students to further develop empathy for others alongside their own problem solving skills within a supportive framework
- to encourage students to consider and practice a range of strategies for coping with stress and to consequently reduce current stress levels and anxieties
- to increase student's level of confidence in social interactions and in their own abilities to cope with stressful situations and conflicts in an assertive and positive way.

It is essential to create a positive mood/tone from the outset and reassure students that this course should be interesting, helpful and fun and will enable them to feel more positive and in control of their own lives and situations.

Setting up Group Rules

This activity is crucial in terms of both setting such a positive tone and ensuring the safety and comfort of all involved in this programme. Students need to discuss and agree their own rules so as to ensure ownership and real agreement to adhere to them throughout each of the ensuing sessions. These rules may well include some of the following:

- we will think and concentrate in each session so that we can all contribute
- we won't laugh at others or put them down
- we'll listen to other's ideas and show respect
- we won't talk over each other
- we'll keep our conversations private to the group
- we'll co-operate with each other
- people can choose not to say things if they don't feel up to it.

Clearly the course tutor(s) will need to be explicit about what it is not appropriate to discuss within this context i.e. any situation which appears to be putting a student at risk should be discussed in a 1:1 meeting with the course tutor. Disclosure of abuse of any kind would need to be dealt with via the usual support system within the school.

Individual Stress Profile

The Stress Profile is set out in the form of a simple questionnaire in which students are required to rate themselves against a series of stressful behaviours and symptoms, identifying if each statement applies to them:

All of the time
Most of the time
Sometimes
Rarely
Never.

The symptoms described cover a range of emotional, physical and behavioural indicators such as:

- feeling moody; upset; anxious and irritated
- headaches and poor sleep patterns
- tiredness, illness, loss of appetite
- feeling undermined, lacking in confidence; depressed
- feeling angry, worthless, lonely and isolated
- self abusive i.e. too much alcohol, food, cigarettes, drugs
- difficulties maintaining positive relationships
- feeling nervous, frightened and over-emotional
- biting nails, getting rashes, having nightmares and aching muscles
- arguing with friends and family and withdrawing from their support.

If students are experiencing these symptoms for the majority of the time then they are clearly experiencing an unhealthy level of stress. Rather than inducing panic about this, the Stress Profile encourages them to focus on the benefits of following this course i.e. they should be able to visualise their lives without these stresses and be able to develop the strategies necessary to cope more effectively with them.

Stress Target Sheet and Contract to Change

The first strategy is made explicit in this activity; don't attempt to change everything in one go! This will only increase the level of stress in your life and result in failure! Students are encouraged to reflect upon their responses and to identify the three things that they currently feel most stressed about and would really like to change. Targets or aims should be realistic and referring back to the Anti-Stress Plan formulated in the Introductory Session may prompt students at this point to further reflect on their targets.

Finally, students are required to sign the Contract of Change and to commit themselves to learning and practising the new skills and strategies introduced in the course. There is an important symbolic message here and it is vital to highlight that they are entering upon a contract to change their current behaviours and feelings about themselves and their lives. To achieve success in this requires honesty, bravery and a genuine commitment and this needs to be reinforced and valued publicly by the course tutor(s).

Resources

The following resources will be needed for this session:

- a quiet room with adequate seating and tables
- pens, pencils, rubbers, sharpeners etc.
- 45 minutes -1 hour to run the session
- a photocopy of the Group Rules format enlarged to A3 size to enable the course tutor(s) to record student's responses

- A4 copies of the Group Rules format for students to record these rules for their own files/use
- a photocopy of the Individual Stress Profile for each student
- a photocopy of the Stress Target Sheet and Contract to Change for each student
- special files/folders for each student in which they can present all the course handouts and activity sheets. This record of work will also aid students in reflecting upon their progress and skills development on a regular basis as well as evaluating personal progress and course content at the end of the course.

Our Group Rules

Our Group Rules for the Strictly Stress Course are:

-

-

-

-

-

-

Individual Stress Profile

Initial Questionnaire

Completed by   _____

Year group   _____

Individual Stress Profile page 1

How stressed do you feel? Complete the questionnaire to find out by ticking the relevant box.

Do you...	All of the time	Most of the time	Sometimes	Rarely	Never
Feel upset and moody?					
Get migraines/headaches?					
Find it hard to concentrate?					
Sleep badly?					
Stop seeing friends?					
Get irritated about things?					
Feel very anxious?					
Take time off school?					
Feel fed up?					
Think that things are all your fault?					
Feel tired?					
Feel physically sick and wound up?					
Eat too much?					
Lose your appetite?					
Get annoyed with members of your family/friends?					
Feel that things are pointless?					
Feel that you just can't cope?					
Get very angry?					
Feel undermined by others?					
Lack confidence?					
Feel isolated/lonely?					
Feel that you are worthless?					

Individual Stress Profile page 2

Do you...	All of the time	Most of the time	Sometimes	Rarely	Never
Stop seeing your friends?					
Smoke/drink too much?					
Feel nervous?					
Keep your problems a secret?					
Argue with friends and family?					
Find it hard to make a decision?					
Feel frightened?					
Burst into tears?					
Feel dependent upon drugs?					
Get muscle ache?					
Feel sad?					
Feel 'butterflies' in your stomach?					
Forget things?					
Bite your nails?					
Get rashes?					
Feel a lump in your throat?					
Feel that your hands are sweating?					
Find yourself clenching your fists?					
Have nightmares, bad dreams?					

If the majority of your ticks are in the first 3 columns then you are probably experiencing an unhealthy level of stress in your life.

You will benefit from this course, which focuses on developing personal self-help strategies to manage stress effectively.

Stress Target Sheet & Contract to Change

Look back at your Individual Stress Profile.
Identify three things that make you feel most stressed and that you would like to change.

Stressor 1.

Stressor 2.

Stressor 3.

How do you currently cope/what do you do to try and handle each of these stressors?

1.

2.

3.

If you would like to cope more efficiently and change and improve your coping strategies, please sign the contract to change.

Contract to Change:

I will try to cope more positively with my stress and to change by learning and using the new skills introduced in this course.

Signed   date

STRICTLY STRESS

Session 2

- ◆ What is Stress?
- ◆ Stress Cards
- ◆ Making distinctions
- ◆ Observing others

Group Session 45 minutes - 1 hour

Brainstorming - What is Stress

This session begins with a brainstorming activity in which students identify the causes of stress and begin to develop personal and general definitions. It is important to encourage students to express their ideas in their own language in order to ensure ownership and usefulness of the activity. Students may wish to work in pairs or small groups prior to feeding back via a whole group discussion at the end of this part of the session. The course tutor(s) could pull all the ideas together, making use of an A3 version of the Brainstorming sheet and highlighting any differences and similarities in responses. It is important to identify the wide range of stressors and causes of stress in people's lives and the fact that some situations may be stressful to all individuals e.g. death of a parent or sibling whilst other stressors may be more person specific e.g. exams or Christmas!

Previous student responses might have included the following:

- stress in feeling insecure, lonely or isolated
- it is when you feel you can't cope with life and things are getting on top of you
- it's when you feel irritated and snap at people because you can't cope with your life
- when you have too much work and can't cope with it all
- when you keep getting headaches because you're worrying about the future
- when you have to start something new or meet new people and you feel that you can't cope
- when people are poor and can't pay their bills
- if someone dies in your family and you just miss them so much
- when you are sent to the head
- if you have exams and you haven't done enough work
- when you have a bad row with your Mum or Dad
- if you know that a teacher doesn't like you and is trying to wind you up
- when you feel pressurised to do drugs or have sex when you don't want to
- if your Mum and Dad fight and split up
- when you are being bullied.

Stress Cards

This activity requires students to study a list of stressful situations and to rank order these stating which is the most stressful and why. It might be helpful to divide the group into smaller subgroups of 3/4 students to allow for discussion regarding their individual responses. They should consider if stress is actually 'different' for each individual person i.e. person specific? Do we all get stressed if we have to much work to do or do some people thrive on a heavy workload? Would one person's workload be too stressful for another and vice versa? Do we have an individual optimum stress level? Do certain stressors such as a death or being bullied affect all individuals in a similar way? It may be helpful to write up such a series of trigger questions on a whiteboard in order to further prompt this small group discussion. Students may have ranked the situations in a similar fashion but there should be differences which need to be highlighted and discussed. The Stress Cards sheet could be photocopied onto card and students can cut out the individual statements prior to rank ordering them. The situations include:

- changing your school/job
- getting divorced
- a row with your Mum /Dad /member of your family
- having no money
- going on holiday
- talking to the Head Teacher /Boss
- chatting to someone of the opposite sex
- getting married
- death of a close friend or member of the family
- leaving school
- Christmas
- being bullied /intimidated by your boss /teacher
- waiting in a queue for a bus /to pay for shopping
- performing in front of an audience
- driving a car
- tidying up
- thinking about school /work.

Making Distinctions

This activity is intended to reinforce the person specific nature of stress and the fact that some people may thrive /appear to thrive on certain stressors. Also, it aims to highlight the fact that some stressors may be enjoyable whilst others may not be enjoyable. Making such a distinction should prompt students to reconsider the nature of stress and the fact that some stressors will present a balance of enjoyment and anxiety e.g. Christmas! Students are asked to identify 2 lists: enjoyable and unenjoyable stressors and to consider the following points / questions:

- is there agreement on the content of the 2 lists
- are the lists interchangeable? (e.g. could taking an exam be an enjoyable stressor for one person and an unenjoyable stressor for another?)
- do specific conditions make a difference? (e.g. the amount of revision that you've done or if the 'right' questions appear on the paper!)

Again, it may be useful to ask students to initially tackle this activity in pairs and to then feedback to the group as a whole. This would allow the course tutor(s) to ensure that the above points are covered fully.

Observing Others

The aim of the final activity in this session is to encourage students to develop their own skills of observation in identifying elements of stress in other's lives. They are asked to look at a range of 'Case Studies' and to then record what they perceive to be the main stressors and the main effects of those stressors in the lives of each of the 4 characters introduced via these sheets. They are then asked to provide advice to each character and it is suggested that students work in pairs or smaller groups on this. It is important to ensure that there is adequate time for discussion and for each student to justify their own views. They will need to consider the consequences of implementing the given advice for each of the characters. The course tutor(s) could facilitate a final discussion, drawing together student's ideas and contributions and highlighting any advice which would appear to be the most constructive and useful. Students may, at this point, be unable to articulate specific stress management strategies - many of which will be covered during the Course. However, what is important is that they are given the opportunity to problem solve in the smaller group context and that course tutor(s) reinforce one of the central aims of the course; 'to develop joint problem solving skills within a supportive framework! As individuals, we may not have all the answers now - but we can certainly work together in order to support each other in determining possible future answers and solutions.

Resources

The following resources will be needed for this session:

- a quiet room with adequate seating and tables
- pens, pencils, rubbers, sharpeners and scissors etc.
- 45 mins - 1 hr to run the session
- student's files in which to present worksheets
- photocopies of the 'What is Stress?' brainstorming sheet for each student
- an A3 copy of the brainstorming sheet 'What is Stress?' to enable the Course tutor(s) to record the whole group's responses
- photocopies of the 'Stress Cards' (onto A4 card) for each student to cut out and rank order
- photocopies of the 'Making Distinctions' sheet for each student
- photocopies of the 'Observing Others' sheets for each student
- large sheets of paper/flip chart for course tutor(s) use as required.

Brainstorm

What is Stress?

What causes Stress?

Work in a small group/pair and identify the nature and causes of stress.

Stress Cards

Changing your school/job	Having no money
Death of a close friend or member of the family	A row with your Mum/Dad/ member of your family
Marriage	Leaving school
Getting divorced	Christmas
Pressure to take drugs	Pressure to have sex
Being bullied or intimidated by your boss/a teacher	Waiting in a queue for a bus/to pay for shopping
Going on holiday	Talking to the Head Teacher/Boss
Performing in front of an audience	Chatting to someone of the opposite sex
Driving a car	Tidying up
Thinking about school/work	Exams and Assessments

Rank these situations - Which is most stressful and why? Discuss your responses in a group and consider if stress is 'different' for each individual. Is stress person - specific? (i.e. what stresses one person may not stress another)?

Making Distinctions

Some people enjoy stress and some people thrive on certain stressors. Work with a partner and brainstorm the following 2 lists:

Enjoyable Stressors	Unenjoyable Stressors
e.g. Christmas with the family	e.g. Taking an exam

Do you agree on the content of these 2 lists? Are the lists interchangeable? For example, could taking an exam be an enjoyable stressor for one person and an unenjoyable stressor for another person? Do specific conditions make a difference? E.g. how much revision you've done/if the 'right' questions came up?

Session 2 - Observing Others

Think about these characters. Can you identify the main stressors in their lives? How will these stressors affect them?

Zoe Banks		Main Stressors
The Scene Zoe's Dad recently left home to go and live with his new girlfriend. Her Mum is really depressed and has stopped going into work. The house is a mess and Zoe is getting worried about her Mum and about her little brother Daniel. He's started to 'act up' at school and the teachers have asked to see her Mum about him. Zoe wants to see her Dad but she's frightened of upsetting her Mum and making the situation worse.		**Main effects on Zoe**
		What would you advise?

Joshua Gambon		Main Stressors
The Scene Joshua has just started at a new school and is finding it quite hard as three boys in his new Form have started calling him fat. He doesn't want to say anything to his Mum as he was bullied at his last school and she'll just go over the top about it and make it worse. She was diagnosed with diabetes 2 months ago and she is still upset about that. He worries about her getting ill but tries to help her round the house and doesn't say anything that might worry or upset her.		**Main effects on Joshua**
		What would you advise?

Zahina Ahmed		Main Stressors
The Scene Zahina recently came to England from India in order to get married. She spends most of her time cleaning and cooking for her new family. Her mother-in-law is constantly criticizing everything that she does and told her that she shouldn't bother trying to find a job as a teacher - it was a waste of time trying to continue to have a career. She said she needed to just have babies and settle down. Zahina feels tense and worried all the time but she's too scared to criticise her mother-in-law to her husband and she has no friends to talk to.		**Main effects on Zahina** **What would you advise?**
Terence Dailey		**Main Stressors**
The Scene Terence is 14 years old. His Dad died when he was 12. He feels that he needs to take on more responsibility, as he is the eldest. He tends to look after his 3 younger brothers a lot, helping them with their school work and cooking their meals each night. His Mum has a part-time job in the evenings and they really need her wages, as money is tight. Terence feels left out at school because he can never go out with his mates in the evening. He still misses his Dad and cries at night, but he can't tell his Mum about it, as she would just worry.		**Main effects on Terence** **What would you advise?**

STRICTLY STRESS

Session 3

- ♦ What makes us feel stressed?
- ♦ How do we cope? Positive and negative reactions
- ♦ Role Play Cards

Group Session 45 mins - 1 hour

Brainstorming - What makes us feel stressed?
In order to begin to develop personal self-help strategies, students need to identify their own stressors. As stress is person-specific and, to some extent, 'age' specific, it will be important to clarify the kinds of stress that young people have to cope with both in and out of the school context. This should then enable students to formulate positive responses in a joint problem solving process which is both empowering to the individuals concerned and encourages further development of empathy and reflective skills. Students responses to this question have included the following:

- teachers giving us too much work
- parents arguing
- falling out with your friends
- being bullied
- getting behind with Course work
- boyfriends/girlfriends
- taking drugs/smoking
- having to buy the 'right' clothes when you don't have much money
- parents splitting up
- my nan dying
- feeling fat and ugly
- when other people have more than you do
- if you can't understand the work and you can't tell the teacher
- your Mum's new boyfriend is horrible and really bossy
- my Dad being out of work and having no money
- exams
- having unprotected sex and worrying about being pregnant
- being labelled by teachers
- people calling me a slag for sleeping with my boyfriend
- cussing/ fights and arguments in class
- teachers who shout and won't explain the work properly
- when people are racist
- thinking about the future and getting a job
- my whole family
- my Mum always putting me down and saying I'm not as clever as other kids
- getting bad grades
- when teachers send letters home to say I've been bad and then my Dad goes mad at me
- teachers showing you up and calling you thick
- not being able to get a girlfriend
- people not fancying me
- having no bust
- my spots/ acne
- when people label you for how you look or speak.

How do we Cope?

Following on from this brainstorming activity, students can identify the 6 common types of stress that students experience both in and out of the school context. It is highly likely that these will include the following:

- stress from parents /family
- stress from teachers

46

- stress from peer group
- stress from personal relationships
- stress from schoolwork /exams
- stress from physical/emotional changes resulting from puberty.

It may be helpful for the course tutor(s) to write this list onto a white board/ large sheet of paper and to give students the opportunity to categorise their own responses in this way. The main aim of the activity is to then identify what would be the positive and negative responses to each stressor. An example is provided on the worksheet as follows:

The Stressor   You have been off sick and have missed a lot of work. The subject teachers are getting at you to complete it all. You feel you can't cope.

Positive Reaction   Talk to a friend
                        Tell your Mum /Dad/Carer
                        Make a proper timetable
                        Keep your timetable
                        Ask for help.

Negative Reaction   Don't go into school
                        Lie to yourself
                        Don't ask for help
                        Go out with friends and don't bother.

Students can feed back their ideas to the group and give reasons as to their categorisation of responses. It will be important to highlight the possible consequences of both negative and positive reactions to the stressors. A key element in developing positive responses and strategies towards coping with stress is to be able to consider the consequences of our behaviours and attitudes and to plan ahead to ensure the best/most positive outcome. The final activity of the session reinforces this point and encourages students to co-operate further in the problem solving process.

Role Play Cards
A range of stressful scenarios are presented on these cards and it would be a good idea to negotiate with students in order to ensure that each smaller group (2-3 students) has an opportunity to 'act out' 2 or 3 of these scenes i.e. each group doesn't present the same scenarios. During the initial discussion and planning of the scenes it will be important to encourage students to identify the following:

- the major stressor
- the negative response - what wouldn't solve the problem or even make it worse
- the positive response - what might alleviate the problem or even solve it
- the 'who', 'when' and 'how' of this plan of action.

It is vital that students begin to perceive themselves as problem solvers who can plan appropriate and positive responses to a range of stressors. Also, this activity should highlight the importance of peer group support and the ways in which friends and relatives can provide useful and constructive advice and support - they are one of the most valuable tools in any stress survival kit!

Adequate time should be allocated to allow each group to present their scenarios and it may also be useful to video these scenes for future reference. Students could then watch this piece of work towards the end of the course and discuss how they might change their responses in the light of what they have learnt during these sessions.

Resources

The following resources will be needed for this session:

- a quiet room with adequate seating and tables
- pens, pencils, rubbers, sharpeners etc.
- 45 minutes - 1 hour to run the session
- student's files in which to present worksheets
- photocopies of the 'What makes us feel stressed?' brainstorming worksheet for each student
- photocopies of the 'How do we Cope?' worksheet for each student
- photocopies of the Role Play Cards for each student
- large sheets of paper /flip chart for course tutor(s) to use as required
- a video camera (as required).

Brainstorm

What makes us feel stressed?

Work in a small group/pair and identify the kinds of stress that students may experience both in and out of school.

How do we cope?

Identify 6 common types of stress that students experience both in and out of school. Then complete the following chart, working out both positive and negative reactions to these situations. An example is provided.

The Stressor **Example**	Positive reaction	Negative reaction
You have been off sick and you've missed a lot of work. The subject teachers are getting at you to complete it all. You feel you can't cope.	✔ Talk to a friend. ✔ Tell your Mum/Dad/Carer ✔ Make a proper timetable. ✔ Keep to your timetable. ✔ Ask for help.	✖ Don't go into school. ✖ Lie to yourself. ✖ Don't ask for help. ✖ Go out with friends and don't bother.
1)		
2)		
3)		
4)		
5)		
6)		

Role Play Cards

Act out the following scenario. Formulate 2 scenes, which show:

   (a) A positive response to the stress.

   (b) A negative response to the stress.

You are getting behind with your homework and feeling like not bothering. The pressure is just too much.

Your Mum and Dad keep arguing and say they are going to split up. You feel hurt, upset and stressed by this.

You've been invited to a friend's party but you don't have anything decent to wear. Your Mum said she can't give you any more pocket money.

Your friend is putting pressure on you to smoke when you go out. You don't want to but you also don't want to be different to the rest of the group.

Your Mum has to work late and leaves you to collect your younger sisters from school. You have to make them dinner, run them a bath and put them to bed. You feel too tired to do your homework.

The Science Teacher is constantly picking on you and trying to show you up in front of the rest of the class. You just feel like not going to these lessons.

Role Play Cards continued

Your Mum has remarried and you can't stand your Step-Dad. He is always getting at you and criticizing everything you do.

People at school are picking on you and teasing you for being slightly overweight. It is getting worse each day that you go in.

Everyone in your form is getting a mobile phone. Your Dad has said you can't have one until Christmas (which is 6 months away). Your friends are making you feel left out and spend all their time phoning each other.

You are feeling pressured into having sex with your boyfriend/ girlfriend. You don't want to because you don't feel ready but everyone else says they're doing it.

Your Gran died 3 months ago. You really miss her as you used to stay with her every weekend. She had cancer. You're worried that your Mum will get cancer as you heard her talking about it. You can't stop worrying or crying at night.

Your Dad lost his job 2 months ago and is in debt. He and your Mum keep arguing about it. You feel frightened that this will break them up. Also they've now had a red reminder for both the gas and electricity bills.

Role Play Cards continued

You've got exams coming up and you are really behind in the 2 subjects that you find hard anyway. You feel like throwing all the hard work you've done in the past into the bin and just not bothering. The 2 teachers concerned say that you are just lazy.

It's coming up for Christmas and everyone is talking about the presents that they will buy each other. You don't have much money and can't afford much for your friends. You're frightened that they will laugh at the small presents you have been able to afford.

Your friends keep falling out and asking you to take sides. They fall out over stupid things and you get stressed by them and are feeling totally torn between the two of them.

There is one teacher who keeps asking you to read out loud in class and has told you that you have to read something in a special celebration assembly next week. You feel that you can't do it. You have a slight stutter and you are worried it will get worse. You feel nervous and stressed at the thought of this.

You are finding French incredibly difficult and can't seem to memorize the vocabulary and verbs. You have a test coming up for both speaking and writing. You feel like bunking off school that day.

You are going to live with your Dad in the opposite end of town as your Mum is moving abroad to live with her new partner. You've got to go into Year 10 in a new school and you are worried sick about being able to cope with all the changes.

STRICTLY STRESS

Session 4

- ◆ What is a true friend?
- ◆ My Circle of Friends and Social Support
- ◆ Advice Page

Group Session 45 minutes - 1 hour

Brainstorming - What is a True Friend?
This activity reinforces the notion of friends as providers of emotional and practical support in times of stress (previously highlighted in Session 3). Students are encouraged to work in a pair or smaller group in order to pool their ideas which may well include some of the following definitions:

- someone who doesn't let you down
- someone who can keep your secrets
- someone who tries to help you find solutions
- someone who loves you
- someone who wants the very best for you
- someone who will really listen
- someone who won't judge you if you've done something wrong
- someone who will tell you the truth
- someone who always tries to help you
- someone who can say they are sorry or admit they are wrong
- someone who accepts you as you are
- someone who will share their feelings and plans with you.

Students can feedback their responses to the whole group and these could be recorded by the course tutor(s) either on an A3 version of the brainstorming sheet or on a flipchart/ larger sheet of paper. It may be useful to highlight any agreements or disagreements as to what constitutes a 'true' friend and to also consider the possibility (or otherwise) of any friend achieving a state of perfection! Being a 'true' friend may be more to do with trying to do the best that you can and being able to admit to defeat or mistakes. Attempting perfection or expecting perfection can themselves be a cause of stress for many of us.

My Circle of Friends and Social Support
This activity is designed to highlight the fact that every individual will have some kind of circle of social and emotional support on which they can draw upon during times of stress and within the course of their everyday lives. This circle may include a wide range of individuals from intimate peers to 'professional' adult supporters. Students are asked to identify their own concentric circle beginning with their closest and most intimate friends in the inner circle and working out towards those who may support them but remain less well known to them e.g. doctor, teacher etc. Family members will not necessarily be included in the inner circle for all students and course tutor(s) will need to be sensitive towards students whose levels of stress are linked to these relationships or who have difficulties in identifying close friends who can and do support them. It will be important to emphasise the quality rather than the quantity of the supporters!

Stress Problem Page - be a true friend
Being and having a good or true friend and maintaining positive and supportive relationships are essential requirements for coping effectively with stress. A central role of the friend is to listen and to offer both emotional and practical support. Talking through the problem identifying positive and negative responses and attempting to formulate solutions is clearly the job of the 'true' friend and these are skills that we can all learn or further develop.

The Stress Problem Page provides students with an opportunity to consider a range of problems and to work co-operatively in formulating considered and useful responses. The 4 problems detail some common and less common stressors:

- aggression / violence from a parent
- arguments with a sibling
- bereavement and the change in role for the eldest child
- bullying which is rooted in homophobia.

Clearly, course tutor(s) will need to be sensitive to individual student's needs and current situations. Students should not feel pressured in anyway to identify personal stressors or to select a problem which might be similar to one with which they're currently dealing. The central aim of this activity is not to address any significant needs of the students but rather to reinforce the importance of sharing resources and ideas in order to help and support each other and to emphasise how everyone can make a contribution to such a process. Making use of 'imaginary' scenarios is a useful means of allowing students to practice and develop these skills in a 'safe' way. Once each pair/small group has formulated a response (making use of the Advice Page worksheet), they can feedback to the rest of the group. course tutor(s) can highlight useful courses of action and the most helpful and constructive pieces of advice - will naturally be advice that clearly focuses upon the consequences of any action, showing the need to think and plan ahead before acting.

Resources
The following resources will be needed for this session:

- a quiet room with adequate seating and tables
- pens, pencils, rubbers, sharpeners etc.
- 45 minutes - 1 hour to run the session
- students files in which to present worksheets
- photocopies of the 'What is a 'true' Friend?' brainstorming sheet for each student
- photocopies of 'My Circle of Friends and Social Support' for each student
- photocopies of the 'Stress Problem Page' for each student
- an A3 version of the brainstorming sheet 'What is a true friend' for course tutor(s)/a flip chart or large sheets of paper on which to record /group ideas / responses (as required).

Someone who gives you
emotional support

Brainstorm

What is a
'true' friend?
List your definitions.

Someone you can confide
in when you feel stressed

Work in a small group/pair and identify the qualities of a true/close friend.

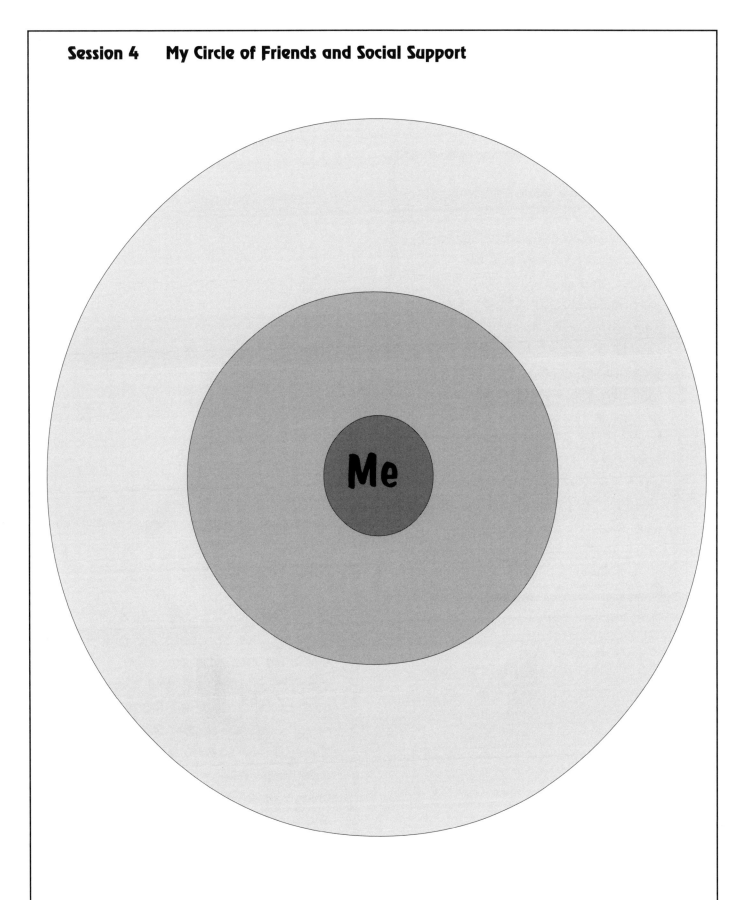

Record the names of your closest and most supportive friends in the inner circle and work outwards in order to list those who may support you but remain less well known to you. E.g. doctor, teacher etc.

<u>Remember! Friends can and do support us when we are stressed.</u>

Stress Problem Page
Be a True Friend

Dear Problem Page,

I'm getting really stressed and quite scared. My Dad has always had a bad temper but just recently has become more aggressive and violent. He shouts a lot at us (which I can just about cope with) but last week he hit my older brother and gave him a black eye and broke 2 of his ribs. We said he'd been in a fight when we went to the hospital. What should I do? I can't go on living like this.

Yours, Megan

Dear Problem Page,

My sister and I are always arguing. She stresses me out because she has to have everything just so' and I'm not like that. I like my mess and I never lose anything. She say's I'm just a scruffy, lazy boy and keeps nagging me to pick things up or tidy things away. She's not all bad. She can be good fun when she relaxes but at the moment she's not allowing either of us to relax. How can I talk to her? What should I say?

Yours, Ben.

Dear Problem Page,

My Mum died three years ago when I was 12. My Dad has relied on me ever since to do all the things she used to do - like cooking, shopping and cleaning. He always gives me £20 on a Saturday so I feel a bit guilty complaining but the trouble is that it's starting to interfere with my schoolwork. After I've cooked, washed up, tidied up and set the table for the next day, I'm shattered. Now that it is Year 10 we are starting our exam courses I'm frightened I'll fail everything. How can I tell Dad? I'm so nervous about it and I can't sleep now.

Yours, Chantelle

Dear Problem Page,

I feel like running away from school on a daily basis. Every time I go into my form room I'm met with comments and remarks from 1 particular group. They are making my life a misery. They say these things under their breath and come up really close and whisper them in my ear and they always do it when the teacher can't see/hear. I don't know why they've chosen to pick on me. They constantly call me 'gay boy' but I'm not gay - even if I was, I don't think they should do that to me. I don't know what to do. I'm frightened that I won't be listened to if I tell and that my friends will just laugh and make a joke of it.

Yours, Daniel.

Advice Page

What advice will you give? Work in pairs and small groups and think carefully about all the possible courses of action you could take in your role as a true friend. Try to identify the best ways to deal with the stressors. Write back.

Dear _____

_____

_____

_____

_____

_____

_____

_____

_____

_____

_____

_____

_____

_____

Yours _____

STRICTLY STRESS

Session 5

- ♦ What makes a healthy life-style?
- ♦ Healthy options
- ♦ Quiz: How healthy are you?
- ♦ Healthy Targets

Group Session 45 minutes - 1 hour

Brainstorming - What makes a healthy lifestyle?

Keeping ourselves fit and healthy equips us better for coping with life's challenges and the potentially stressful situations that we may encounter on a daily basis. It is consequently vital that students understand what is meant by a healthy lifestyle in order to then be able to make informed choices as to how they can maintain their own physical and emotional health. It will be particularly important to highlight the positive effects of exercise in terms of alleviating stress and promoting a balanced emotional state. Being truly healthy does, however, require attention to both the physical and emotional sides and it should also again be emphasised that having a positive and optimistic outlook which is supported by good friends and relatives is also an essential factor in ensuring a healthy lifestyle. This initial brainstorming activity aims to elicit student's views as to what makes a healthy lifestyle. They are encouraged to work in a pair or small group in order to brainstorm ideas. These may include some of the following:

- eating good food and cutting out junk food
- taking exercise regularly
- not smoking/ taking drugs
- not drinking too much alcohol
- sleeping enough
- not having too much stress
- being able to cope with problems
- having nice times when you can relax
- feeling positive
- talking about problems rather than keeping worries to yourself
- not having too many things to do at once i.e. being organised each day
- having friends you can rely on.

Students can feedback their responses to the whole group and these could then be recorded by the course tutor(s) either on an A3 version of the brainstorming sheet or on a flip chart/larger sheet of paper. Hopefully, there should be some agreement as to what constitutes a healthy lifestyle and it may well be worth allocating some time to discuss the negative effects of substance abuse, bad diet and lack of exercise as appropriate.

Healthy Options

This activity requires students to rank order a list of statements in terms of being the most and least healthy options. The statements are presented on A4 card and students can cut out the 20 options prior to arranging them in rank order. There is no 'right' way of presenting the cards i.e. some students may wish to place 2 or 3 statements on the same level if they think these have equal status or importance to maintaining good health. In order to encourage students to justify their own views and options it is suggested that this activity is completed individually prior to students pairing up and comparing their sequences. The statements presented are as follows:

- eating fibre each day
- not getting anxious about things
- not eating sweets
- eating a low fat diet

- not smoking or taking drugs
- going on holiday
- eating fruit and vegetables
- having a 'proper' breakfast
- sleeping for 7-9 hours per night
- taking regular exercise
- being able to relax
- having good friends
- eating at regular times
- being optimistic
- liking other people
- being the 'right' weight for your height
- having lots of money
- enjoying hobbies
- feeling happy
- not eating junk food.

Again, this paired discussion is likely to highlight the person-specific nature of stress and, to some extent, our ways of coping effectively with it. For example, going on holiday may be so stressful for some people that it will not be rated highly as a healthy option and some people may not actually need 7 - 9 hours sleep per night in order to feel alert and healthy. However, there may also be clear agreement on the dangers of smoking and high fat diets since the available medical evidence can hardly be refuted!

How Healthy Are You Quiz

Students finally complete the quiz 'How healthy are you?' in order to determine their own state of physical and emotional health and to then identify 3 personal targets / things that they can do in order to improve both their health and their ability to cope more effectively with stress. Although this is presented as a 'fun' activity in the style of a Teen Magazine Quiz, the purpose is serious in terms of promoting students to make personal changes for the better. What is important is to ensure that any personal target goals are realistic, manageable and achievable. Unrealistic targets will only result in additional stress which is clearly not what is required!

Students may wish to share their personal health goals at the end of the session. The course tutor(s) should assess the situation sensitively in order to decide if this would be appropriate and useful for all involved.

Resources

The following resources will be needed for this session:

- a quiet room with adequate seating and tables
- pens, pencils, rubbers, sharpeners, scissors etc.
- 45 minutes - 1 hour to run the session
- student's files in which to present worksheets
- photocopies of the 'What makes a healthy lifestyle?' worksheet for each student
- an A3 photocopy of the 'What makes a healthy lifestyle?' for course tutor(s)/a flip chart or large sheets of paper on which to record group responses (as required)

- photocopies of the 'Healthy Options' worksheet for each student. (These will need to be A4 thin card)
- photocopies of the 'Quiz: How healthy are you?' for each student
- photocopies of the 'Healthy Tagets' for each student.

Brainstorm

What makes
a healthy
life-style?

Work in a pair/as a member of a small group in order to clarify the ways in which we can maintain a healthy life-style.

Healthy Options

Cut out these statements and then sort them into order in terms of the most healthy options and the least healthy options.

Taking regular exercise	Not eating junk food
Sleeping for 7-9 hours a night	Feeling happy
Eating a 'proper' breakfast	Enjoying hobbies
Eating fruit and vegetables	Having lots of money
Not smoking or taking drugs	Liking other people
Eating a low-fat diet	Being optimistic
Not eating sweets	Eating at regular times
Having good friends	Going on holiday
Eating fibre each day	Being able to relax
Being the 'right' weight for your height	Not getting anxious about things

Compare your sequence with a friend. Do you agree on what constitutes a healthy life-style? Can you justify your ideas?

How Healthy are You?

Complete the following questions. Then work out your score in order to assess how healthy you are!

SCORING SYSTEM
(a) answers = 3 points
(b) answers = 2 points
(c) answers = 1 point

Personal Statement	Underline Your Choice	Points
I take exercise	(a) Frequently (b) Sometimes (c) Hardly ever	
I feel anxious and nervous about things	(a) Hardly ever (b) Sometimes (c) Often	
I sleep about	(a) 7-9 hours a night (b) 5-7 hours a night (c) Under 5 hours a night	
I eat junk food	(a) Rarely (b) About once/twice a week (c) At least 3 times a week	
I smoke	(a) Never (b) Sometimes (c) Everyday	
I drink alcohol	(a) Rarely (b) Sometimes (c) Often	
I get aggressive	(a) Rarely (b) Sometimes (c) Frequently	

Sub total =

Personal Statement	Underline Your Choice	Points
I feel that I have supportive friends	(a) All the time (b) Sometimes (c) Frequently	
I feel very angry	(a) Rarely (b) Occasionally (c) Often	
I know that I am the 'right' weight for my height	(a) All the time (b) Sometimes (c) Never	
I feel positive about myself	(a) everyday (b) sometimes (c) never	
I feel fed up and depressed	(a) Rarely (b) Sometimes (c) Often	
I eat sweets	(a) Rarely (b) Sometimes (c) Often	
I feel optimistic about the future	(a) Most days (b) Some days (c) Hardly ever	
I can 'chill out' and relax	(a) Anytime (b) Sometimes (c) Hardly ever	
I have a good laugh	(a) Often (b) Sometimes (c) Rarely	

Sub total =

Personal Statement	Underline Your Choice	Points
I can talk about my problems to my friends	(a) Anytime (b) Sometimes (c) Hardly ever	
I feel unorganised	(a) Rarely (b) Sometimes (c) All the time	
I can manage my time well	(a) Most of the time (b) Sometimes (c) Rarely	
I can concentrate effectively	(a) Most of the time (b) Sometimes (c) Hardly ever	

Sub total   =

Total page 1   =

Total page 2   =

Total page 3   =

Total Score   =

How Healthy are You?

Scoring

20 - 30 Unhealthy

You are not very healthy at all! It's time now to make some significant changes, in the way you eat, exercise and generally look after yourself. Sit down and take some time to make a plan of action. Set yourself 3 realistic targets, which will ensure that you take better care of yourself and cope more effectively with stress.
Go for it!

31 - 46 Quite Healthy

You are able to keep yourself healthy and cope reasonably well with most of the stress that you encounter. However, you sometimes lapse into a self-indulgent mood and give in to your unhealthy cravings! Try to adjust the balance so that you offset any lapses with a greater proportion of healthy eating, exercise and sleep. Take time off to sort out a new more disciplined routine. Set 3 targets.
Go for it!

47 - 60 Totally Healthy

You are certainly healthy and well able to maintain a good routine in order to counteract daily stress levels. You know how to keep fit, eat well, rest and make the best use of the emotional support offered by friends. You generally feel positive about your life. Perhaps you can investigate new sports and activities and incorporate these into your routine also you can think more about how you can support your friends. Set some new goals.
Go for it!

Session 5

Healthy targets

Try to think of 3 things you can do in order to improve:
a) Your health.
b) Your ability to cope with stress.

3 things I can do to improve my health are:

1)	2)	3)

3 things I can do to improve my ability to cope with stress are:

1)	2)	3)

STRICTLY STRESS

Session 6

- ♦ 3 brainstorms - working out the differences between assertive, passive and aggressive behaviours
- ♦ Self -evaluate Quiz
- ♦ Act it out - practising assertive behaviours
- ♦ Observing assertive behaviours

Group Session 45 minutes - 1 hour

Brainstorming - working out the differences between assertive, passive and aggressive behaviours

In order to cope positively and effectively with stress it is necessary to reflect upon our own responses and behaviours in order to determine how assertive we are or need to be - particularly in our dealings with others. Aggressive and passive responses may indicate a high level of personal stress (alongside low levels of confidence and self-esteem) and may often engender stress and angry feelings in others - consequently making a bad situation far worse. Knowing what is meant by being assertive and practising such behaviours is a key strategy in terms of maintaining a healthy and relatively stress free existence. Being able to say 'no' in a positive manner - whether to pressure from friends or to unreasonable demands from teachers or parents - is central to keeping such a balance.

This initial brainstorming activity requires students to work in pairs or small groups in order to define what is meant by assertive, passive and aggressive behaviours. It may be useful to have dictionaries available as a prompt to this activity. However, it is important that students actually articulate their own views and ideas in their own language in order to truly comprehend these distinctions and to begin to identify the types of responses that will both increase and decrease stress.

Students definitions have previously included the following:

Assertive

- saying what you want
- being clear but not loud
- listening to other people but not letting them talk over you
- showing and giving respect.

Passive

- not saying enough
- mumbling and being too quiet
- letting people abuse you
- not doing what you really want to do.

Aggressive

- being really loud and mouthy
- pushing other people around and bullying them
- not listening to other people
- showing other people up in a bad way.

It will be helpful to ask each pair/group to feedback in order to highlight any agreements or disagreements regarding these distinctions and to also encourage students to further discuss why and how each response might cause or reduce stress levels in particular situations/individuals.

Self-evaluate - Quiz

This activity is designed to encourage students to further reflect upon their own behaviours and responses. How aggressive are they? Do their aggressive behaviours result in lower or higher levels of stress both for themselves for those around them? Do they want to be able to behave more assertively in order to reduce anxiety and stress levels and how can they achieve such a goal? The quiz is set out in 3 parts and intended for private use by individuals i.e. no brainstorming or paired work here! It is important to stress the need for honest responses. It is impossible to affect change if there is no basis in reality to begin from.

Students are asked to tick or cross against a series of statements which detail both assertive (Part 1) and aggressive (Part 2) behaviours. In part 3 of the Quiz they are then encouraged to consider the consequences of both kinds of behaviours i.e. what usually happens when you have been behaving in an aggressive / assertive way? The students are then required to state which of these behaviours cause them to feel most stressed and anxious and to then identify 3 situations in which they'd like to behave more assertively. Part 3 of a female student's form was completed as follows:

a) <u>What usually happens when you have been behaving in an aggressive way?</u>
I get angry and shout. It's usually when my Mum nags me or my teacher tells me off in front of my friends. I shout back and get more angry. Sometimes I storm out and ignore them. Then I'll get a detention.

b) <u>What usually happens when you have been behaving in an assertive way?</u>
I say what I want to say but I don't shout it out. Sometimes I'll ask my Mum to stop. If I ignore the teacher it can help and I'll get into less trouble. I don't get upset and feel angry for the whole day if I say how I feel in the first place.

c) <u>Which behaviour causes you to feel more anxious/stressed? Why?</u>
When I'm aggressive. It doesn't get sorted out and I feel upset for too long. People just think I'm bad.

d) <u>Identify 3 situations in which you would like to respond more assertively and state how you will behave at these times:</u>

1. When my Mum moans at me for not doing enough work. I'll tell her I'm trying my best and show her my work so she'll stop.
2. When the maths teacher shows me up I'll ignore it and I'll tell my Form Tutor to tell him to stop.
3. When people laugh at my fat stomach I'll just tell them to stop as they're showing themselves up for what they really are.

Act it Out - practising assertive behaviours

It is not always easy to behave in an assertive way - even when you know it will reduce your stress levels and probably produce a more positive outcome. This is particularly true if you have got into a habit of responding to certain situations or stressors in a passive or aggressive way. However, in order to change such behaviours, students need to be encouraged to be honest and reflective and to be given opportunities to actually 'practice' assertive behaviours and responses. This series of 10 problem situations is designed to give students the chance to 'act out' both assertive and aggressive responses. Each scenario requires students to work out 2 conversations - one in which they respond assertively to the character who is causing/has caused the problem/stress and one in which they respond aggressively. Students can swop roles so as to give everyone a chance to practice these skills.

It may be useful to video these scenes for future reference. Allow students to further review each other's performances via use of the Observing Assertive Behaviours Checklist.

Observing Assertive Behaviours Checklist

Students can make use of this checklist in reviewing each other's scenes. This will once again reinforce the distinction between assertive and aggressive behaviours and enable students to support each other in further developing their skills. Time will need to be allocated for this discussion at the end of each 'performance'. However, this will be earlier if scenes are recorded as the course tutor(s) will then be able to stop the video tape at the appropriate time and also allow students to 're-watch' particularly useful scenes where there is clear evidence of assertive behaviours /positive role model etc.

Resources

The following resources will be needed for this session:

- a quiet room with adequate seating and tables
- pens, pencils, rubbers, sharpeners etc.
- 45 minutes - 1 hour to run the session
- student's files in which to present worksheets
- photocopies of the Brainstorming sheet 'Working out the differences between assertive, passive and aggressive behaviours' for each student
- an A3 photocopy of the Brainstorming sheet/a flip chart or large sheets of paper on which course tutor(s) can record group responses (as required)
- a copy of the Self-evaluate Quiz for each student
- copies of the Act it Out - practising assertive behaviours sheet for each student
- copies of the Observing Assertive Behaviours Checklist for each student (no. of copies will be equivalent to the number of scenes performed)
- video recorder and television (as required).

3 Brainstorms!
Work out the difference

What is 'being assertive'?

What is 'being passive'?

What is 'being aggressive'?

Work in pairs/small groups and try and describe these behaviours. Which response is likely to cause the most stress and which is likely to cause the least? Give your reasons.

Session 6   Self Evaluate Part 1

How assertive are you? Tick against the statements which apply to you. Think carefully and be honest.

I listen properly to others and show respect for their views and feelings. =====

I am honest with myself about how I feel and how I think about things. =====

I am sensitive towards other people and I can tell how they are feeling. =====

I am honest with others about my thoughts and feelings. =====

I can calmly ask for things that I want. =====

I will take responsibility for my behaviours and the choices that I make. =====

I know my rights and I know that others have such rights. =====

I don't need others to tell me how brilliant I am all the time. =====

Session 6   Self Evaluate Part 2

How aggressive are you? Again tick against the statements which apply to you. Think carefully and be honest.

I sometimes verbally abuse other people.   =====.

I sometimes physically abuse other people.   =====.

I can cause others to feel upset and unhappy.   =====.

I am 'loud'.   =====.

I have to win even if other people get hurt in the process.   =====.

I put others down.   =====.

I can be very sarcastic.   =====.

I can sometimes intimidate or bully others into doing things that they don't really want to do.   =====.

Session 6   Self Evaluate Part 3

Think carefully and try to answer the following questions:

(a)   What usually happens when you have been behaving in an aggressive way?

_____

_____

_____

(b)   What usually happens when you have been behaving in an assertive way?

_____

_____

_____

(c)   Which behaviour causes you to feel more anxious/stressed? Why?

_____

_____

_____

(d)   Identify 3 situations in which you would like to respond more assertively and state how you will behave at these times:

1.   _____

2.   _____

3.   _____

Have a go! Try out your strategies!
Remember! Saying 'NO' is a way of being assertive.

Practising Assertive Behaviours
ACT IT OUT!
Rehearse!   Model!
Practice!   Prepare!

Role play assertive and aggressive responses to each situation.
Use the Observing Assertive Behaviour Checklist in order to assess your
friend's performances!

---

1) Your friend wants you to bunk off school and you know that this will get you into trouble.

2) You've done all the work on a joint research project. Your partner has been really lazy and you feel fed-up.

3) Your Mum always interrupts you when you are talking. She just can't listen for more than 10 seconds.

4) Your friend is so nosey. She always wants to know your business and then tells it to everyone who'll listen. You're really mad about this.

5) Your P.E. teacher is constantly making sarcastic remarks about you being overweight. You feel embarrassed hurt and angry.

6) A Year 11 student is constantly pushing you out of the way when you try and queue up in the sweet shop after school.

7) Your boyfriend/girlfriend is constantly comparing you to a former boyfriend/girlfriend. This makes you feel nervous and insecure.

8) You have been given a double detention for throwing rubbish around the room in the French lesson – BUT – it really wasn't you!

9) You seem to be doing all the clearing up, cleaning and tidying at home. Your elder brother and sister are both at work and say they don't have time to help. You're getting fed up and need to tackle your Mum.

10) Your friend is always borrowing things from you – clothes, magazines and money. You are getting fed up, as you are now owed over £40. You need to sort this out.

Session 6

Observing Assertive Behaviours
Checklist

Use the following check – list. How many assertive behaviours can you observe? How many aggressive behaviours can you also identify?

Name of Actor ....

Observer ....

Date ....

Tick/highlight the behaviour you observe in the scene!
Watch Carefully!

Gives clear reasons	☐	Uses sarcasm	☐
Maintains eye-contact	☐	Uses put-downs	☐
Acknowledges the other's viewpoint	☐	Uses a loud voice and speaks quickly	☐
Uses a calm and gentle voice	☐	Giggles/laughs nervously	☐
Waits and listens carefully to responses	☐	Appears confused and unclear	☐
Keeps body still and relaxed	☐	Fidgets a lot	☐

Did you observe more assertive or more aggressive behaviour? What do you think the Actor needs to work on now?

STRICTLY STRESS

Session 7

- When and why do we need to be organised?
- Prioritising
- Plan your day and manage your time
- Sorting Sam

Group Session 45 minutes - 1 hour

brainstorming - When and why do we need to be organised?

Being disorganised can result in unmanageable levels of stress - both in and out of the school context. Students need to be able to particularly manage their work loads and set and keep to relative targets if they are to achieve success. Effective time management and the ability to organise a balanced personal timetable which allows for both leisure and work activities are essential if stress is to be kept to a minimum. Again, there is an emphasis in this session on maintaining an appropriate balance and the fact that this may well be person-specific. Priorities may be different for each student, but the need to organise schoolwork and leisure effectively in order to achieve personal goals with the minimum of stress, should be a central priority for all the students on the course.

This initial brainstorming activity requires students to work in pairs or smaller groups in order to identify the times that they need to be organised and the reasons why it is necessary to organise their time in this way. Previously, students contributions have included the following:

- to get my homework in on time
- not to get a build up of course work and then rush it and do badly at the last minute
- so I can still go to football training 4 times a week
- to stop my Mum nagging me
- when it's exam time and you need to revise 10 subjects
- so I can still go out with my mates in the evening
- to remember stuff for school like my Games kit
- I can find stuff in my room
- I can stop work and go out
- to stop you getting worried and behind.

Prioritising

A key skill that students need to develop is that of prioritising - not just workload but also leisure and relaxation activities. If 5 subjects are given as homework on a Monday and 2 have to be handed in on the Wednesday and the other 3 on the Friday of that week, it should be relatively easy to plan the homework timetable for the week. Clearly, you would prioritise the 2 subjects to be handed in on the Wednesday and wouldn't simply pick out the most interesting/fun piece of work to do first, disregarding the deadlines. Should you want to go to Football training 3 times a week and see this as a priority in terms of your health and emotional well being, these sessions would need to be time-tabled into the week's events as a priority alongside other activities and tasks. Trying to fit 'everything' into a day and not prioritising and planning effectively will simply result in higher levels of stress and much unfinished work.

This activity requires students to plan their own day by formulating 3 lists as follows:

- Important things that have to be done
- Important things which I can wait to do
- Things which are not very important.

One student's lists were as follows:

Important things that have to be done:

- going to school
- tidy my bedroom
- having a shower
- doing my homework
- eating meals
- listening to music.

Important things which I can wait to do:

- phoning a good friend
- visit a friend
- watch TV
- chat to my parents
- go out in the evening
- have a rest.

Things which are not very important:

- play on my computer
- read a book
- go shopping
- reading a magazine.

Students can feedback their Priorities Lists to the group as a whole and the course tutor(s) can highlight differences and similarities. What is essential is for each individual to know their own needs and priorities and not to be concerned if these are different to others in the group. Just as stress is person-specific so are our priorities. For example, one student may 'have' to listen to music on a daily basis in order to relax and switch off from work or worries whilst another student would prefer to watch a TV Soap or play football.

Plan your day and manage your time

This activity reinforces the need to prioritise on a daily basis whilst also suggesting that this can be done even more effectively if there are specific times allocated to each activity. For example, if you have planned to watch TV for one hour after school prior to completing your homework but then decide to watch 2 more programmes there will obviously be less time for this work and it will probably not be of the best quality. You may then also not have time to go to the gym or to take the dog for a walk - the pressures and stresses will simply mount up and you'll end up feeling as though you've achieved very little. Planning activities into a 'timed' timetable is one method of avoiding such situations.

Students are asked to list 10 things that they would like to achieve during the following day and to then record these in a day's timetable which consists of hourly slots from 7.00am to 12.00 midnight. They will obviously need to take this timetable home to then complete the Evaluation: Did you manage to complete the most important activities? If not, how could you have been better organised? It is important to stress the solution focused nature of this task - if you didn't get everything done then how could you do better next time? Visualising a better future and the development of skills is a priority. Students should not feel that they have simply failed. This, after all, may well be a new skill and will certainly be a strategy that each student can continue to develop and work on.

Sorting Sam

Students are finally asked to transfer this skill of prioritising to another situation i.e., to help to plan another student's week. The activity could be completed in pairs so as to allow for more discussion and to again reinforce how our priorities are clearly person-specific. However, it will be important to emphasise that everyone's timetable will need to ensure a good balance between school, homework, leisure and rest if they are to maintain a healthy and relatively stress-free existence. Students are encouraged to try out this strategy for themselves over the coming week and it would be useful to allow some feedback time at the start of Session 8 to enable students to evaluate this strategy and to discuss the extent to which it hopefully helped them to achieve more and to be better organised.

Resources

The following resources will be needed for this session:

- a quiet room with adequate seating and tables
- pens, pencils, rubbers, sharpeners etc.
- 45 minutes - 1 hour to run the session
- student's files in which to present worksheets
- photocopies of the Brainstorming sheet 'When and why do we need to be organised?' for each student
- an A3 copy of the Brainstorming sheet/a flip chart or large sheets of paper on which course tutor(s) can record student responses as a whole (as required)
- photocopies of the 'Prioritising' worksheet for each student
- photocopies of the 'Plan your Day and Manage your Time' worksheet for each student
- photocopies of the 'Sorting Sam' worksheet for each student.

Brainstorm

When and why do we need to be organised?

Work in a pair/as a member of a small group in order to identify the times that we need to be organised and the reasons why we need to organise our time.

Session 7 **Prioritising**

Plan your day! Highlight the activities that you have to do each weekday. Then complete the priorities list.

Phoning a good friend

Eating meals

Listening to music

Reading a magazine

Going to school

Having a shower

Have a rest

Read a book

Tidy my bedroom

Watch TV.

Go shopping

Go out in the evening

Chat to my parents

Visit a friend

Doing my homework

Play on my computer

Priorities List		
Important things that have to be done	Important things which I can wait to do	Things which are not very important

Plan Your Day

and manage your time!

List the things that you want to achieve tomorrow:

1	
2	
3	
4	
5	
6	
7	
8	
9	
10	

Tick against the most important activities – your priorities! Then plan these into your day in your 'days' plan.

REFLECT AND REVIEW

Did you manage to complete the most important activities?

If not how could you have been better organised?

_____

_____

_____

_____

My Day's Plan
7.00am
8.00am
9.00am
10.00am
11.00am
12.00 noon
1.00pm
2.00pm
3.00pm
4.00pm
5.00pm
6.00pm
7.00pm
8.00pm
9.00pm
10.00pm
11.00pm
12.00 Midnight

Sorting Sam

Sam has to do many different things during the week. These are listed on his notepad. How would you draw up his timetable to ensure a good balance between school, homework, leisure and rest?

* Eat meals
* Watch TV
* Attend lessons
* Phone his best friends
* Go to the Youth Club
* Help Mum do the garden

* Do homework
* Visit his Gran
* Go to the gym
* Visit the library
* Play tennis
* Cook 2 of the evening meals

* Practise guitar
* Tidy his room
* Write to his penfriend
* Listen to music
* Go to football club
* Do his own ironing

Time	Monday	Tuesday	Wednesday	Thursday	Friday
7.00am					
8.00am					
9.00am					
10.00am					
11.00am					
12.00 noon					
1.00pm					
2.00pm					
3.00pm					
4.00pm					
5.00pm					
6.00pm					
7.00pm					
8.00pm					
9.00pm					
10.00pm					
11.00pm					
12.00 midnight					

Try this out for yourself! Plan your own week and see if this strategy helps you to achieve more and be better organised.

STRICTLY STRESS

Session 8

- ◆ When and how can we relax?
- ◆ My Haven
- ◆ A Relaxation Script
- ◆ My Relaxation Timetable

Group Session 45 minutes - 1 hour

Brainstorming - When and how can we relax?

Being able to relax and to actually 'feel' relaxed is essential in terms of maintaining a healthy and relatively stress free lifestyle. Managing stress effectively is crucial to each individual's well being and relaxation strategies and opportunities to relax need to be a central part of any stress management programme/individual's lifestyle. Clearly, there needs to be an appropriate balance between both stress and relaxation levels and these will again be person-specific to some extent. How and when we relax will be a matter of choice but that fact that we all need periods of relaxation and relaxation strategies to draw upon in times of stress is not open to debate. This session highlights this fact alongside introducing some specific relaxation strategies for students to try out for themselves.

The Brainstorming activity requires students to work in a pair or as a member of a small group in order to identify when they may need to relax and the strategies that they currently make use of in order to do so. Students past responses have included the following:

- going out with my friends
- watching TV
- listening to music
- yoga
- swimming
- playing football
- having a hot drink before I go to sleep
- having a bath
- playing on my computer
- lie on my bed
- thinking positively before I go into the exam room
- taking deep breaths and calming down before I start the exam paper
- reading a book to help me sleep
- going to the gym for a workout
- going out for a walk
- having a drink
- when I've had a bad day at school and been in trouble I need to relax
- smoking
- eating 'comfort' food
- going round the shops
- going jogging
- tidying my room
- phoning my friend
- daydreaming
- drawing
- going on the Internet.

It will be important to not only note similarities and differences in student's responses but to also discuss the particular merits or negative aspects of certain strategies. For example, smoking may well enable you to feel instantly 'relaxed' but as with alcohol, this drug will also act as a stimulant and have a negative effect on stress levels or sleep patterns in the longer term (besides causing major respiratory problems). Alternatively, having a bath may be a positive means of relaxing for most people whilst relaxing via tidying up or organising things may be a more person-specific strategy! The course tutor(s) will need to again reinforce this person specific element and to reinforce the importance of being able to both identify and make use of your own strategies in order to relax and consequently achieve a balanced, healthy lifestyle in which stress is managed effectively.

My Haven

This activity requires students to use their imaginations in order to visualise a personal Haven - a place in which they can find real peace and feel truly relaxed. This place can be somewhere which actually exists such as a holiday venue, a specific room, a beach etc. or a totally imagined venue where they know they'd be able to achieve this state of mind. Students are asked to describe this place making use of words or pictures or both - as appropriate. It would be useful to ask each individual to then share their 'Haven' with the group as a whole and for the course tutor(s) to highlight similarities i.e., conditions which may be common to each description. These may include some of the following:

- quiet, peaceful atmosphere
- warmth
- positive feelings e.g. happiness
- stillness
- lack of anxiety
- restful qualities
- cool colours / warm colours
- gentle sounds
- feelings of love and security
- no arguments/ confrontation
- stress free
- tranquillity
- slow moving
- safe and protected
- contentment
- comfortable at all times
- no negative feelings/happenings
- feeling in control
- escape
- beautiful environment.

A Relaxation Script

Following on from this Visualisation strategy, students will next be introduced to a relaxation script and given the opportunity to make use of this within the group context. It is suggested that the course tutor(s) explain how such scripts are of use and how they can be used as required by each student in the privacy of their own rooms at home. It would be helpful if the course tutor(s) read the script aloud as students followed each of the 16 points in turn. Initially there may be a few giggles or moments of embarrassment but these should soon diminish with a sensitive and calm approach from the course tutor(s)!

My Relaxation Timetable

The final activity in this session requires each student to formulate an individual Relaxation Timetable for a period of 1 week. Students are provided with a list of relaxation strategies to choose from but they should also be encouraged to make use of their own strategies if they wish to. Suggested strategies include:

- yoga
- meditation
- quiet room time
- taking gentle exercise
- muscle tension exercises
- listening to music
- visualisation
- relaxation script
- taking a nap
- deep breathing.

Students are asked to decide if they need to allocate the same time each day for this exercise or to consider using their strategies at various times throughout each day. They are encouraged to try out a different strategy each day and to then evaluate how successful this was in terms of aiding the relaxation process by awarding a mark out of 10 for each of the strategies tried. They are finally asked to highlight the reasons for the success of the best /most useful strategy and to identify anything else that they feel might help them to relax further. It may be useful to allow for some feedback time regarding this activity at the start of Session 9 in order to allow students to highlight the best or most useful relaxation strategies. Again, this will probably also reinforce how relaxation and the use of relaxation strategies is person-specific.

Resources
The following resources will be needed for this session:

- a quiet room with adequate seating and tables
- pens, pencils, rubbers, sharpeners etc.
- 45 minutes - 1 hour to run the session
- student's files in which to present worksheets
- photocopies of the Brainstorming sheet 'When and how can we relax' for each student
- an A3 photocopy of the Brainstorming sheet /a flip chart or large sheet of paper on which course tutor(s) can record student responses as a whole (as required)
- photocopies of the 'My Haven' worksheet for each student
- photocopies of 'A Relaxation Script' for each student
- photocopies of 'My Relaxation Timetable' for each student.

Brainstorm

**When and how can
we relax?**

Work in a pair/as a member of a small group in order to identify when you
need to relax and how you can do this. Compare your ideas and note
similarities and differences. Do we all relax in the same way? In what ways
are we different?

My Haven

Let your imagination run free.

Relax and calmly let your mind wander to a place of real peace. A special place – A Haven for you.

Visualise a place where you will feel safe, peaceful and able to completely relax. This could be a special room, a place that you have visited and loved for it's peace and security or an imaginary place – somewhere that you know will be a special haven to you.

Describe this place. Use words, pictures or both!

This is my Haven ....

Session 8

A Relaxation Script

Prepare

You'll need to be in a quiet room with no distractions. Sit in a chair with both feet planted firmly on the ground and legs uncrossed. Put your hands in your lap, close your eyes and off you go!

1. Clench your fists - hold them, feel the tension, then let your fingers loose and relax. Feel yourself relax all over. Then repeat.

2. Bend from your elbows and tense up your biceps. Feel the tension, then put your arms out and let them relax. Repeat. Really feel the tension and the relaxation in your muscles.

3. Straighten up your arms so that you feel the tension in the upper parts - within the muscles on the backs of your arms. Then let your arms hang loose and feel the tension disappear. Repeat.

4. Close your eyes extremely tightly. Feel the tension in your eyelids and around your eye sockets. Then relax your eyes - still keeping them closed and enjoy the sensation. Repeat.

5. Frown and pull the muscles in your forehead together. Then relax and feel your forehead becoming smooth and relaxed. Repeat.

6. Clench your fists tightly. Relax and open your lips a little. Repeat.

7. Close your lips together tightly. Then relax and focus on the difference between the relaxed position and the tensed position. Feel yourself relax all over your face, in your mouth and in your throat. Repeat.

8. Lift your head up and let it drop back as far as you can (without any straining). Feel the tension in your neck. Move your head from left to right and right to left, feeling the tension moving into each side of your neck. Next lift your head forwards and press your chin downwards against your chest. Then return you head to an upright position and relax. Repeat.

9 Lift your shoulders up and hold in the tension then drop and relax. Feel this relaxation spreading to your back and all the parts of your face and neck. Repeat.

 10 Concentrate on relaxing your whole body and breath slowly in and out. Each time you exhale imagine all the tension leaving your body. Next breath in, inhale deeply and hold your breath. Then breath out feeling your chest relax. Breath in deeply through your nose counting slowly to five. Then exhale slowly, letting your breath free to the count of five. Repeat.

 11 Next, tighten up your stomach muscles. Hold your stomach in as tightly as you can and then let the muscles relax. Concentrate on the two different sensations of tension ad relaxation. Next push your stomach out and hold in this position prior to relaxing the muscles again. Repeat.

 12 Tighten up your thighs and buttocks and then release and relax. Press down on your heels and then relax. Repeat.

 13 Press your feet into the floor and feel your calf-muscles tensing. Release and relax. Repeat.

 14 Bend up your ankles towards your body and hold them tightly. Then release and feel them relax. Repeat.

 15 Curl up your toes as tightly as you can. Hold them tightly. Relax and release them. Repeat.

 16 Finally, let yourself relax all over - from your toes, through your feet, ankles, calves, shins, knees, thighs, hips, stomach and lower back. Feel the tension escape. Relax your upper back, chest, shoulder, arms and fingers. Feel your neck, jaws and facial muscles relax. Breath in deeply and then slowly let your breath out. Count slowly from 1- 10 and then open your eyes. You are now truly relaxed.

My Relaxation Timetable

Look, Think & Reflect
Choose your strategies

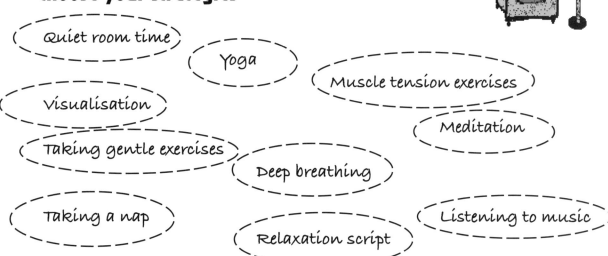

Quiet room time

Yoga

Muscle tension exercises

Visualisation

Meditation

Taking gentle exercises

Deep breathing

Taking a nap

Listening to music

Relaxation script

Draw up a Relaxation Timetable for 1 week. Decide if you need to allocate the same time each day for this exercise or if you want to use your strategies at various times. Choose a different strategy for each day and then evaluate how successful it has been in helping you to relax by awarding each session a rating out of 10.

E.g. 1 = not successful   5 = quite successful   10 = totally successful

Sunday	Monday	Tuesday	Wednesday	Thursday	Friday	Saturday
Time:	Time:	Time:	Time:	Time:	Time:	Time:
Strategy used:	Strategy used:	Strategy used:	Strategy used:	Strategy used:	Strategy used:	Strategy used:
Rating:	Rating:	Rating:	Rating:	Rating:	Rating:	Rating:
—— 10	—— 10	—— 10	—— 10	—— 10	—— 10	—— 10

The most successful strategy was _____

I think that this was because _____

Other things that might help me relax might be _____

STRICTLY STRESS

Session 9

- ◆ Stress - Solving the Problem
- ◆ Problem solve stress that needs to be managed
- ◆ Stress Problem Solving Format

Group Session 45 minutes - 1 hour

Stress - Solving the Problem

This worksheet reinforces 4 basic ways /methods for handling stress effectively. It would be useful to discuss these prior to asking students to complete the activity sheet. The course tutor(s) could make use of a flip chart/whiteboard, in order to record students ideas and contributions under each of the headings:

Show your feelings
Nurture yourself
Problem solve
Actively get distracted.

The examples provided on the worksheet should clarify what each strategy may entail but students will also want to make their own contributions. Again, this will highlight the person-specific nature of stress management. Student's past contributions have included the following:

Show your feelings

tell your Mum how you are feeling
talk to your friend about your feelings
have a scream in the privacy of your bedroom
cry
sing
shout
write down your feelings in a diary or poem.

Nurture yourself

go to the cinema and watch a film to escape
buy yourself some new clothes
have a bath
read your favourite book
watch your favourite TV programme
eat nice food
have some chocolate
have a drink.

Problem solve

write out the problem and brainstorm some solutions
think about the causes and work out where the stress is coming from - change what you are doing
assert yourself and say how you feel and what you think
work out some strategies with a friend
plan out what you can do and write down your plan - stick to it and try again if it doesn't work
try all the strategies until one works.

Actively get distracted

> go to the gym and workout
> go for a long run
> play football/tennis/basketball
> learn a new skill
> find a new computer game and try it out.

Students are asked to identify a stressful time /situation when they might be able to make use of each of these strategies and to clarify exactly what they would do in order to cope more effectively. It is important to emphasise the need to ensure a balance between these strategies and not to become over reliant upon one single method of handling stress. Each situation will demand a slightly different approach and students need to develop confidence in working out which response is going to be most effective in any given situation.

Problem solve - stress that needs to be managed

This is the first of 2 activities which aim to encourage students to adopt a 'stepped' approach towards handling stress and 'problem solving' stressful situations. This problem solving strategy has 7 steps as follows:

> identifying / articulating 'my stressor'
> saying how I feel
> listing the symptoms I am currently experiencing
> identifying how this affects those around me
> what I do now i.e., what is my behaviour like in terms of responding to this stress?
> what are the current outcomes?
> working with a friend in order to identify how I can manage this stress more
>   effectively.

An example of how a completed exercise which could be presented to students prior to the start of the activity, is as follows:

My stressor
My Mum and Dad are splitting up.

How I feel
Angry worried and upset.

My symptoms
I can't sleep and I can't keep up with my homework.

How others are affected
My Mum cries a lot and they are both worried about me. My Dad isn't at home much.

What I do
I hide in my room. I don't talk and just escape into my music. I shut my Parents out.

The outcomes

No one is talking and we all just shout. When we're all in Mum is really stressed and Dad has got a new flat

Brainstorm with a friend

I can go out and walk to clear my head. Stop shutting them out and talk to them about how I feel and they feel. We can listen to each other. Plan ahead so I know I can see them both.

This strategy clearly promotes the use of a logical step by step approach to problem solving stress alongside reinforcing the importance and value of peer support. This solution focused strategy does not allow the sharing process to become an entirely negative whinge! The structure encourages students to articulate specific symptoms and outcomes and to then identify a more positive way forward.

Students are finally asked to Role Play a 'before' and 'after' scene. This can be done in a pair /slightly larger group as appropriate and the course tutor(s) will need to ensure that time is allocated to allow students to present and comment upon these scenes.

Stress Problem Solving Format

This second 'stepped' approach to coping more effectively with stress is once again a solution focused design but aims to encourage students to work with even greater independence i.e., formulating their own solutions prior to sharing these with a friend. The 'ICAS' approach is in 4 parts as follows:

Step 1 - **Identification** - This is the stress that I need to manage.

Step 2 - **Clarification** - These are the things that I can change in this situation.

Step 3 - **Articulation** - These are the strategies that I can use in order to change the situation and my response to it.

Step 4 - **Solution** - This is what I will do!

Students are asked to have a go at using this format in order to problem solve a range of stressful situations and are again prompted to maintain a balance of different strategies. When sharing their solutions, they may also like to consider the usefulness of the problem solving strategies introduced in this session i.e., do the 'stepped' approaches promote a more considered and reflective response to stressful situations and prevent students from reacting in an ill-considered/ negative way? Can students identify /formulate more personal stepped approaches to solving the problems of stress?

Resources

The following resources will be needed for this session:

- a quiet room with adequate seating and tables
- pens, pencils, rubbers, sharpeners etc.

- 45 minutes - 1 hour to run the session
- student's files in which to present worksheets
- a flipchart/whiteboard/large sheets of paper for course tutor(s) to record student's responses regarding the initial activity
- photocopies of the 'Stress - Solving the Problem' worksheet for each student
- photocopies of the 'Problem Solve - Stress that needs to be managed' worksheet for each student
- photocopies of the 'Stress - Problem Solving Format' worksheet for each student.

Stress - Solving the Problem
Basic ways to Handle Stress

Show Your Feelings

1 You can talk to a pal, let off steam, sing, write a poem!

Nurture Yourself

2 Have a special treat, spoil yourself and indulge yourself!

Problem Solve

3 Decide what is causing the stress e.g. not becoming assertive, not managing your time. Then make a plan and sort

Actively Get Distracted

4 Do something sporty - get fit and out of breath. Find an exciting hobby and use your brain!

When could you use these strategies? Identify the stressful situation and state how you would deal with it by using each strategy.

1. Showing my feelings	2. Nurturing myself	3. Problem solving	4. Active distraction
When I could do this	When I could do this	When I could do this	When I could do this
What I would do	What I would do	What I would do	What I would do

Try the strategies and keep a balance between the strategies!
Sort the stress!

Problem Solve
Stress that needs to be managed

1 My stressor

_____
_____
_____
_____

2 How I feel

_____
_____
_____
_____

4 How others are affected

_____
_____
_____
_____

3 My symptoms

_____
_____
_____
_____

6 The outcomes

_____
_____
_____
_____

5 What I do

_____
_____
_____
_____

Brainstorm with a friend! Help each other. How could you manage this stress better? Think of the strategies you have learnt. Record your suggestions:

_____
_____
_____
_____

Role-Play a 'Before' and 'After the Advice' scene. Note the Differences.

Stress Problem Solving Format - I.C.A.S.

A Stepped Approach

Step (1) Identification	Step (2) Clarification
This is the stress that I need to manage:	There are the things that I can change in this situation:

Step (3) Articulation	Step (4) Solution
These are the strategies that I can use in order to change the situation and my response to it:	This is what I will do:

Have a go at using this format in order to problem solve a range of stressful situations. Remember to use a balance of different strategies. Share your solutions and compare notes with a friend.

STRICTLY STRESS

Session 10

- ◆ Review your week
- ◆ Analyse your Stressors
- ◆ Stress Busters

Group Session 45 minutes - 1 hour

Review your week

This activity encourages students to further reflect upon their own personal stressors via the formulation of daily Stress O' graphs. Students draw a graph to identify the times that they felt the most and the least stressed. Peaks are drawn to represent the times of most stress and troughs to show the times of least stress. Students are then encouraged to notice any patterns in their experience. This visual tool should enable them to identify the main causes of their stressful moments and to then measure how effectively they were able to cope with each stressor. It will be helpful to allow time for thinking and talking so that students can also identify the specific strategies they have used and consider how they might be able to gain better outcomes for themselves in the future. The emphasis here is to further develop skills of self-reflection alongside highlighting the value and importance of peer support in terms of solving problems. Previously completed Stress O' graphs indicated a range of stressors for individual students throughout each day of the week. These included:

- rows at home
- mealtimes
- getting up in the morning
- rows with friends
- bullying at break /lunchtimes
- being late for school due to erratic levels of public transport
- altercations with subject teachers
- homework issues
- behaviour issues /problems regarding specific subjects
- boyfriends /girlfriends
- difficulties in understanding new concepts in lessons
- going out in the evening
- going to bed
- using the telephone /Internet during the evening.

Discussing the nature and patterns of these stressful moments should also allow students to revise the problem solving /stress management strategies introduced in the Course materials to date. Also it will be important to highlight individual strategies that students may be using which are entirely personal to them i.e., to share their own developing expertise.

Analyse your stressors

This activity provides students with a further opportunity to practice self-reflection and to re-use and make use of the stress management strategies introduced in the course to date. Students are asked to self-rate a list of common stressors as follows:

- behaviour
- weight
- diet
- fashion
- tidiness

- positive outlook
- attitude
- hair style
- punctuality
- the future
- friends
- money
- cleaning room/personal space
- TV
- homework
- relationship.

Clearly, the person specific nature of stress will again be reinforced. Having fashionable clothes may cause some stress to many students, whereas being significantly overweight will probably be the cause of stress for only a minority of students. What is important is that all students can identify their main stressors and the particular people that may be associated with them. The activity finally requires students to identify 4 situations that they'd now like to change and to draw up a plan of action which also includes the stress busting strategies that they might make use of. It will be important to emphasise the need to prioritise stress in this way - attempting to solve too many problems at once will probably simply result in additional stress (which is not the object of the exercise at all). It will also be useful to ensure that students have adequate time to share their plans with a partner and to compare their strategies. Have they really produced the 'best plan' possible or can they advise each other on how to improve these plans still further? Or, do they recognise that what may be the best strategy for them may not be the best strategy for someone else?

Stress Busters

This final problem solving activity encourages students to again collaborate and support each other via formulating a 'Stress Buster' for a range of stress related problems. They are encouraged to make use of a range of practical coping strategies and to state why they think their plan will be successful. Distinguishing between stress that can be prevented and stress that needs to be managed is crucial to this procedure and needs to be reinforced by the course tutor(s). It may be helpful to provide students with a completed 'stress buster' to act as a prompt. For example:

Stressor   My Mum is always nagging me for getting up late and for my room being a total mess.

Stress Buster   You should make a compromise with your Mum and make things on the surface look neat - even if your drawers/cupboards are not too tidy.

                Get an alarm - you will avoid arguments if you can get up on time and stop stressing you Mum. Show her you're making an effort and she'll lay off you. This is stress you can AVOID.

Alternatively,

Stressor   My big brother is such a pain. He's always been good at everything and my Mum calls him her Golden Boy. I just can't do anything right and I hate him for it. My Mum's attitude just stresses me out.

Stress Buster   This is stress that needs to be MANAGED - your brother can't really help being good at everything.

                 Be positive - don't waste your energy on being jealous /hating your brother.

                 Think of the things you can do and show your Mum.

                 Tell your Mum how upset and angry she has made you feel - but do it calmly when you're on your own with her. Let your feelings out to her.

The final part of the activity encourages students to design their own Stress Buster Cards and to share and articulate their strategies. This is a further opportunity to revise and reinforce the strategies introduced in previous sessions and to highlight individual's personal strategies for coping effectively with different stressors.

Resources
The following resources will be needed for this session:

- a quiet room with adequate seating and tables
- pens, pencils, rubbers, sharpeners etc.
- 45 minutes - 1 hour to run the session
- student's files in which to present worksheets
- photocopies of the 'Review your Week' worksheets for each student
- photocopies of the 'Analyse your Stressors' worksheet for each student
- photocopies of the 'Stress Busters' worksheet for each student.

Session 10

Review Your Week

This is Joel's 'Stress o'graph' for last Monday. The peaks show when she felt most stressed and the troughs show when she felt least stressed.

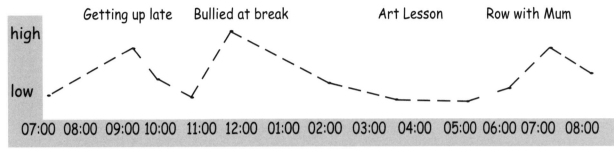

Getting up late   Bullied at break   Art Lesson   Row with Mum

high

low

07:00 08:00 09:00 10:00 11:00 12:00 01:00 02:00 03:00 04:00 05:00 06:00 07:00 08:00

DRAW YOUR STRESS O'GRAPH FOR EACH DAY OF THE WEEK
Label the stressors and the peaceful moments

<u>Monday</u>

high

low

7am| 8am| 9am| 10am| 11am| 12pm| 1pm| 2pm| 3pm| 4pm| 5pm| 6pm| 7pm| 8pm| 9pm|

_____

<u>Tuesday</u>

high

low

7am| 8am| 9am| 10am| 11am| 12pm| 1pm| 2pm| 3pm| 4pm| 5pm| 6pm| 7pm| 8pm| 9pm|

_____

<u>Wednesday</u>

high

low

7am| 8am| 9am| 10am| 11am| 12pm| 1pm| 2pm| 3pm| 4pm| 5pm| 6pm| 7pm| 8pm| 9pm|

_____

<u>Thursday</u>

high

low

7am| 8am| 9am| 10am| 11am| 12pm| 1pm| 2pm| 3pm| 4pm| 5pm| 6pm| 7pm| 8pm| 9pm|

_____

Review Your Week continued

Friday

high

low

7am	8am	9am	10am	11am	12pm	1pm	2pm	3pm	4pm	5pm	6pm	7pm	8pm	9pm

Saturday

high

low

7am	8am	9am	10am	11am	12pm	1pm	2pm	3pm	4pm	5pm	6pm	7pm	8pm	9pm

Sunday

high

low

7am	8am	9am	10am	11am	12pm	1pm	2pm	3pm	4pm	5pm	6pm	7pm	8pm	9pm

THINK ABOUT IT

What were the main causes of your stressful moments?

How effectively did you cope and what strategies did you use?

What would gain you better outcomes in the future?

Analyse Your Stressors

Use the sad faces to indicate the things/situations/people that appear to cause you stress. The code is as follows:

😊 = a small amount of stress 😐 = quite a lot of stress ☹ = far too much stress

Add in any additional stressors and then identify specific people who may contribute to the stress.

Stressors	Code	People I associate with this stress e.g. parent/friend/teacher/sibling
My behaviour		
My weight		
Healthy diet		
Clothes I wear (fashion)		
Keeping tidy		
Being positive		
My attitude		
My hair		
Punctuality		
The future		
Friends		
Money		
Cleaning my room		
T. V.		
Swearing		
Homework		
My relationship		

Identify a maximum of 4 stressful situations that you would now like to change. Make a plan and include the different stress busting strategies you might use e.g. assertion, relaxation techniques, being organised, talking to others etc. Share your plan with a partner and compare strategies. Can you support each other in producing the BEST PLANS?

Stress Busters

Work in a small group and devise a 'Stress Buster' for each of the problems. Try to use a range of coping strategies and be practical! Give reasons for your choice of strategy and say why you think this would be most the successful. Make sure that you distinguish between stress that can actually be prevented and stress that needs to be managed.

Stressor
My Mum is always nagging me for getting up late and for my room being a total mess. It's not neat but I know where to find things.

Stress Buster

Stressor
My best friend is smoking more and more because she's nervous about the SAT's. She's got a bad cough now and won't listen to me when I tell her to stop chain smoking. My Dad died of Cancer and it brings back all the bad feelings for me.

Stress Buster

Stressor
My Maths teacher is putting pressure on me to get up to date with coursework and start revising. I hate Maths and can't be bothered but I'm fed up with the teacher.

Stress Buster

Stressor
My big brother is such a pain. He's always been good at everything and my Mum calls him her Golden Boy. I just can't do anything right and I hate him for it. My Mum's attitude just stresses me out.

Stress Buster

Stressor
My best friend is really depressed because her Nan died. She doesn't want to go out or do anything. I'm feeling fed up as well as I'm lonely and don't know how to help her.

Stress Buster

Stressor
I'm trying to lose weight because my friends now call me a fat cow. I've not been eating properly for 3 weeks now and I haven't lost any weight. I wish they would just leave me alone and that I could stand up to them and say that I'm okay being the the way I am.

Stress Buster

Design your own Stress Buster Cards. Work with a partner and swap cards so that you can devise solutions to each other's stress problems. Again, make use of a range of strategies that you have learned on this course and give your reasons for your choice.

STRICTLY STRESS

Course Review

- ♦ Brainstorm - What do we know about stress and how to manage our stressors?
- ♦ Reflect and Review
- ♦ Evaluate - Questionnaire
- ♦ Strictly Stress Action Plan
- ♦ Certificate of Completion

Group Session 1 hour - 1 hour 30 minutes

Brainstorm - What do we know about stress and how to manage our stressors?

This activity aims to review and reinforce the knowledge and skills that students have gained from the Course as a whole. It is suggested that students initially work as a pair/as part of a small group in order to identify facts and coping strategies prior to sharing and comparing ideas with the whole group. It would be helpful if the course tutor(s) recorded all responses onto a flip chart/enlarged brainstorming sheet as this would not only reinforce the work done to date but also provide a visual record of achievement - gaining such knowledge and skills is certainly something to be celebrated/students responses have previously included the following:

- stress is different for every individual
- changes cause stress
- some stress can be managed while other stressors can be eliminated
- we can help each other cope by talking and giving emotional support
- being healthy can reduce stress
- acting aggressively can increase stress levels and make a stressful situation worse
- being organised helps to reduce stress
- solving problems using step by step strategies can help
- stress is when you can't cope and feel insecure
- you can get physical symptoms when you are stressed
- not having enough money makes you stressed
- too much work causes stress
- being bullied is a stress for most people in schools
- exams cause stress but you can plan ahead and organise yourself a bit more
- family fights cause stress
- if someone dies or leaves you then you'll experience stress - this would be the same for most people
- learning to relax can help to reduce stress
- talking and showing how you feel can help you to solve stress related problems
- not keeping a balance between 'work' and 'play' can make you feel stressed
- being unfit can cause more stress and doing exercise can help you to cope better.

Reflect and Review

This activity is designed to allow each student to review his/her progress in terms of meeting their original targets. Students will need to have access to their files for completed work in order to look at their Stress Target Sheets and Contract to Change from Session 1. This will enable them to evaluate their success in making changes and in developing new coping strategies. It will be useful to highlight the most effective strategies and for students to consider what they might do differently in the future - particularly if success has been limited. It is important, however, that this activity remains solution focused i.e., focuses on the best way forward rather than dwelling on any past failures. Even if some students are unable to identify major successes, they will be able to identify how they have increased their knowledge of stress, it's causes and methods of coping or managing their stressors. Knowing about something is clearly not the equivalent of being able to do it /use it, but it is certainly a step in the right direction!

The final activity on the worksheet requires students to also measure their progress by once again completing the Individual Stress Profile from Session 1. It is important that students do not look at their completed forms from Session 1, but complete the form again prior to then completing both attempts. It is hoped that students will score higher on this second attempt, having increased their knowledge, skills and support structures. However, it may be necessary for the course tutor(s) to provide additional 1:1 support and advice if some individuals continue to experience unhealthy levels of stress which they cannot manage effectively. There will of course be times in all our lives when circumstances change dramatically and when we feel that we have lost control of a situation. Suffering from such a change is not a failure in itself. Being able to recognise, analyse and then plan the way forward within a healthy support structure is the real measure of our success. Denying the existence of the stressor is perhaps the greatest failure.

Evaluate - Questionnaire

This final questionnaire is perhaps one of the most important activities of this kind in the Course as a whole as it allows for both students and the Course Facilitator(s) to evaluate the content, delivery and outcomes of the sessions. In part 1, the students rate themselves, on a scale of 1-10, for meeting the basic objectives of the course and for developing a range of self-help strategies for effective Stress Management. Part 2 of the questionnaire asks students to rate the resources and delivery strategies for how useful they have been, alongside identifying ways in which they would improve the course. This should provide useful feedback to the course tutor(s) and inform the planning of future courses, highlighting the need to modify /adjust the content, resources or style of delivery.

Strictly Stress Action Plan

It is important that students are encouraged to continue to develop the skills they have learnt and to continually reflect upon their progress in terms of coping with stress. This will be the real measure of any success - that the students continue to evaluate and reflect and are able to manage both existing and future stressors effectively.

The Action Plan requires students to identify 3 main areas that they would like to work on/change and the strategies that they will use in order to affect such change. It is vital that they set a review date and identify a significant adult in the school context with whom they can review their progress. Access to a Mentor/ some form of mentoring may well be necessary for some of the students targeted via the Strictly Stress Course. Clearly, these students will need to be identified by the course tutor(s) at this stage and the necessary support structures put into place (with the agreement of students and parents). What is vital is that all students do not see this session simply as the end of the course but rather as the beginning of a new way of thinking about the process of change and self-management. Stress can be managed and students need to see themselves as agents of change who can take control of their own situations. The course tutor(s) should reinforce these points with students at this point.

Certificate of Completion

This certificate could be photocopied onto card and presented to students by the course tutor(s) at the end of the session. It is essential that all students feel included in this celebration and are made aware that their efforts and achievements are valued. It may be helpful to allocate some extra time in order to make this a 'special' occasion, providing refreshments/musicians as appropriate. Everyone should be praised for their achievements and encouraged to continue to support each other in further developing their stress management skills and strategies in the future.

Resources

The following resources will be needed for this session:

- a quiet room with adequate seating and tables
- pens, pencils, rubbers, sharpeners etc.
- 1 hour - 1 hour 30 minutes to run the session
- student's files in which to present worksheets
- a flip chart/ whiteboard/A3 photocopy of the Brainstorming sheet for the course tutor(s) to collate/record the student's responses
- photocopies of the Reflect and Review worksheet for each student
- photocopies of the Individual Stress Profile from Session 1 for each student
- students previously completed Individual Stress Profiles from Session 1
- photocopies of the Evaluation Questionnaire for each student
- photocopies of the Strictly Stress Action Plan for each student
- photocopies (A4 card) of the Certification of Completion for each student signed and dated by the course tutor(s)
- refreshments/music as required.

Brainstorm

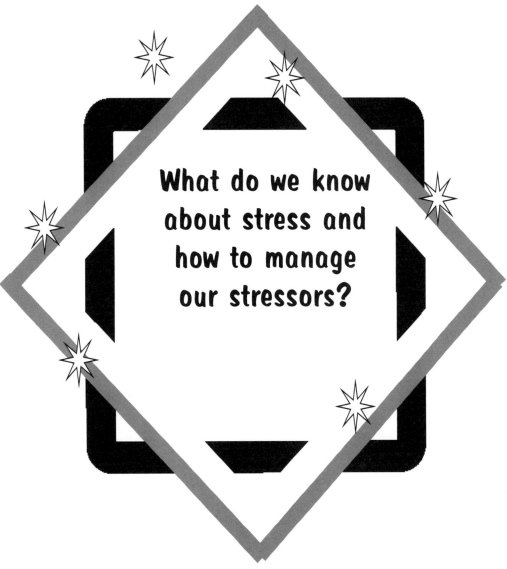

What do we know about stress and how to manage our stressors?

Work in a pair/as a member of a small group in order to identify facts and coping strategies. Try to remember the range of coping strategies that we have covered in this course. Share and compare your ideas with the whole group.

Course Review

Reflect and Review

Look back to your Stress Targets Sheet and Contract to Change from Session 1.
How successful have you been in making changes and coping effectively with your
stressors? Think carefully, identify these stressors once again and then answer the
following questions:

Stressor 1	Stressor 2	Stressor 3

How well have you coped with each of the stressors?

Stressor 1   Very Well ☐   Okay ☐   Not Well ☐

Stressor 2   Very Well ☐   Okay ☐   Not Well ☐

Stressor 3   Very Well ☐   Okay ☐   Not Well ☐

What strategies did you use for
Stressor 1

Stressor 2

Stressor 3

Which of the following strategies was the most effective for you and
why do you think this is so?

How would you cope differently with the stressors? What might you do
differently in the future?

Reflect & Review continued

Now go back to complete the Individual Stress Profile from Session 1. DO NOT look at your completed form from this session, but wait and compare the second go with this first attempt once you've finished your assessment. How have things changed for you?

Share your success in the group.

Course Review

Evaluate

Please complete this final questionnaire in order to provide feedback to the course facilitator(s) and to aid them in planning future courses and session.

Rate the following statements on a scale of 1 - 10

Part 1   YOUR SKILLS

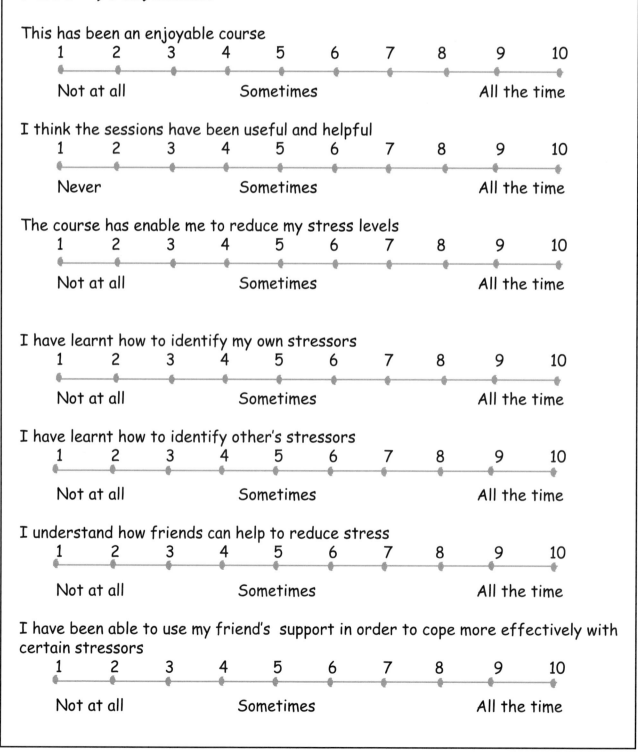

This has been an enjoyable course

| 1 | 2 | 3 | 4 | 5 | 6 | 7 | 8 | 9 | 10 |

Not at all   Sometimes   All the time

I think the sessions have been useful and helpful

| 1 | 2 | 3 | 4 | 5 | 6 | 7 | 8 | 9 | 10 |

Never   Sometimes   All the time

The course has enable me to reduce my stress levels

| 1 | 2 | 3 | 4 | 5 | 6 | 7 | 8 | 9 | 10 |

Not at all   Sometimes   All the time

I have learnt how to identify my own stressors

| 1 | 2 | 3 | 4 | 5 | 6 | 7 | 8 | 9 | 10 |

Not at all   Sometimes   All the time

I have learnt how to identify other's stressors

| 1 | 2 | 3 | 4 | 5 | 6 | 7 | 8 | 9 | 10 |

Not at all   Sometimes   All the time

I understand how friends can help to reduce stress

| 1 | 2 | 3 | 4 | 5 | 6 | 7 | 8 | 9 | 10 |

Not at all   Sometimes   All the time

I have been able to use my friend's support in order to cope more effectively with certain stressors

| 1 | 2 | 3 | 4 | 5 | 6 | 7 | 8 | 9 | 10 |

Not at all   Sometimes   All the time

I understand how keeping healthy can reduce stress

| 1 | 2 | 3 | 4 | 5 | 6 | 7 | 8 | 9 | 10 |

Not at all   Sometimes   All the time

I feel that I have a healthy lifestyle

| 1 | 2 | 3 | 4 | 5 | 6 | 7 | 8 | 9 | 10 |

Not at all   Sometimes   All the time

I understand the distinction between assertion and aggression

| 1 | 2 | 3 | 4 | 5 | 6 | 7 | 8 | 9 | 10 |

Not at all   Sometimes   All the time

I know how to be assertive and can reduce my stress levels in this way

| 1 | 2 | 3 | 4 | 5 | 6 | 7 | 8 | 9 | 10 |

Not at all   Sometimes   All the time

I know that being organised helps to reduce stress

| 1 | 2 | 3 | 4 | 5 | 6 | 7 | 8 | 9 | 10 |

Not at all   Sometimes   All the time

I am organised

| 1 | 2 | 3 | 4 | 5 | 6 | 7 | 8 | 9 | 10 |

Not at all   Sometimes   All the time

I am able to relax by using specific relaxation techniques

| 1 | 2 | 3 | 4 | 5 | 6 | 7 | 8 | 9 | 10 |

Not at all   Sometimes   All the time

I know which relaxation technique to use in particular places/contexts

| 1 | 2 | 3 | 4 | 5 | 6 | 7 | 8 | 9 | 10 |

Not at all   Sometimes   All the time

I understand how to use problem solving strategies in order to reduce stress

| 1 | 2 | 3 | 4 | 5 | 6 | 7 | 8 | 9 | 10 |

Not at all   Sometimes   All the time

I have been able to use problem solving strategies in order to reduce particular stressors

| 1 | 2 | 3 | 4 | 5 | 6 | 7 | 8 | 9 | 10 |

Not at all   Sometimes   All the time

Course Review

The Resouces:

	Not useful			Quite useful			Extremely useful			
1. Worksheets	1	2	3	4	5	6	7	8	9	10
2. Brainstorming Activities	1	2	3	4	5	6	7	8	9	10
3. Role Play	1	2	3	4	5	6	7	8	9	10
4. Use of Stress/Problem Cards	1	2	3	4	5	6	7	8	9	10
5. Questionnaires	1	2	3	4	5	6	7	8	9	10
6. Group Discussion	1	2	3	4	5	6	7	8	9	10
7. Paired Discussion	1	2	3	4	5	6	7	8	9	10
8. Facilitator/Teacher talking	1	2	3	4	5	6	7	8	9	10
9. Using the video to record and review role plays	1	2	3	4	5	6	7	8	9	10
10. Personal Target Sheets, Contract to Change	1	2	3	4	5	6	7	8	9	
11. Comfort and Privacy	1	2	3	4	5	6	7	8	9	10
12. The Evaluation Form	1	2	3	4	5	6	7	8	9	10

I would improve this course by:

_____

_____

_____

_____

Thank you for your help!

Strictly Stress Action Plan
Look to the Future! Be Positive!

Look back at your course

Review and identify 3 main areas that you would still like to work on/ change.

I still need to work on these stressors:

1. ➡️ _____

STRATEGIES that I will use   _____

_____

2. ➡️ _____

STRATEGIES that I will use   _____

_____

3. ➡️ _____

STRATEGIES that I will use   _____

_____

THINK CAREFULLY - WHAT WORKS BEST FOR YOU?

I will review my progress with_____ on _____

I will ask _____ to help me in this process.

MY PROMISE TO MYSELF!
I finally promise to continue to self-evaluate and review my progress in order to manage my stressors effectively.

Signed _____

Date _____

Certificate of Completion

Name

You have successfully completed the
Strictly Stress Course

Well done!
You are a star

Signed

Dated

STRICTLY STRESS

References

References

Appleby(1967) in Bailey, D. & Sprosten, C. (1987) Understanding Stress: HMSO

Butler, G. & Hope, T. (1995) Manage Your Mind: Oxford University Press

Coleman, J. & Hendry, L. (1990) The Nature of Adolescence (2nd Edition): Routledge & Kegan Paul

DfEE (1999) Social Inclusion: Pupil Support

DORE, H. (1990) Coping with Stress: Hamlyn Help Yourself Guide

George, E., Iveson, C., & Rathner, H. (1990) Problem to Solution - Brief Therapy with Individuals and Families: Brief Therapy Press

Jacobson, E. (1983) Progressive Relaxation (2nd Edition): University of Chicago Press

Kyriacon, C. & Butcher, B. (1993) Stress in Year 11 school children: Pastoral Care in Education 11, 19-21

March, J.S. (Ed) (1995) Anxiety Disorders in Children and Adolescents: Guildford Press

Markham, U. (1990) Helping Children Cope with Stress: Sheldon Press

McConnon, S. & McConnon, M. (1992) Stress – A Personal Skills Course for Young People: Thomas Nelson

Miles, S.H. (1992) Helping Pupils to Cope with Stress: Framework Press

Murgatroyd, S. & Woolfe, R. (1982) Coping with Crisis – Understanding and Helping People in Need: Open University Press

Rae, T. (2000) Confidence, Assertiveness, Self-Esteem: Lucky Duck Publishing

Rhodes, J. & Ajmal, Y. (1995) Solution Focused Thinking in Schools. Behaviour, Reading and Organisation: Brief Therapy Press

Robson, M., Cook, P. & Gilliland, J. (1995) Helping Children Manage Stress: British Educational Research Journal, 21. 165-174

Warden, D. & Christie, D. (1997) Teaching Social Behaviour: David Fulton Publishers

Wright, C.L. (1996) The Exam Kit: Letts Educational

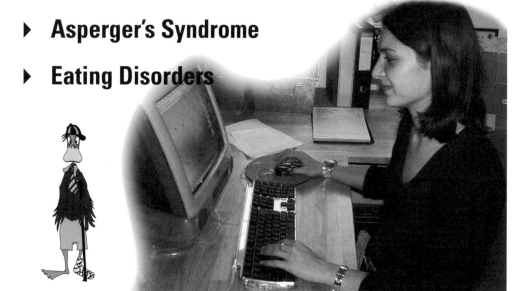